# Armagh

## City of Light and Learning

## Paintings by Joe Hynes
## Text by Maureen Campbell

Cottage

Publications

First published by Cottage Publications,
Donaghadee, N. Ireland 1997.
Copyrights Reserved.
© Illustrations by Joe Hynes 1997.
© Text by Maureen Campbell 1997.
All rights reserved.
No part of this book may be reproduced or stored
on any media without the express written
permission of the publishers.
Design and origination in Northern Ireland.
Printed and bound in Singapore.

ISBN 1 900935 05 8

# The Artist

A native of the City, Joe Hynes has an intimate knowledge and love of Armagh which is reflected in his sensitive treatment of these landscapes.

An established artist, Joe's work has been widely exhibited and may be seen in collections both at home and abroad. A tribute to his universal appeal is the publication of many fine examples of his work as Greeting Cards.

In May 1997, Joe attended the Silver Jubilee Celebrations of the Templeton Prize for Progress in Religion in Westminster Abbey. He witnessed His Royal Highness Prince Philip present the Scroll, which he has illustrated for the past 25 years, to the 1997 recipient Mr. Pandurang Shastri Athavale.

Although perhaps better recognised by his flower paintings, Joe's watercolour landscapes are being increasingly sought after by discerning collectors.

# The Author

Maureen Campbell is a recent past-pupil of Armagh College of Further Education and an Honours Graduate in Communication, Advertising and Marketing (CAM) from the University of Ulster at Jordanstown.

Apart from periods in Liverpool, London, Dublin and Donegal she has lived most of her life in Armagh and is an ex-columnist with both the Ulster Gazette and Armagh Observer.

During 'Armagh Together' 94/95 she was Press and Public Relations Officer for the festival and has since opened her own PR Consultancy, Woodford Communications - the only one of its kind in Armagh.

After winning an award in the prestigious Ian St James Award she has published a number of short stories and is the Chairman of Armagh Writers Group. Maureen lives in Armagh with Roy and their two greyhounds.

# Contents

# Armagh, City of Myth and Legend

The magic of Armagh stems from an ancient past when Ard Macha was the earliest capital of Ulster and the seat of power for Ireland's kings and queens. Archaeological evidence has shown how, 5,000 years ago farmers tilled and worked the land around the grassy slopes that now constitute the city. Pottery, spearheads and other excavated artifacts prove the existence of late Bronze Age and early Iron Age habitation from around 700 B.C., but facts and figures are over-shadowed by the stories of spirit ancestors, gods and goddesses and the legendary heroes and heroines whose exploits have been passed down through generations. From the bards of Iron Age society, through the writings of early Christian monks and by the story-tellers of today, the myths and legends surrounding Ard Macha live on, presenting a technicolour picture of ancient history.

Many stories have been told about the foundation and naming of Armagh ..... but who can say which is true or which has more elements of the truth than others? Did it all begin around 600 B.C. when Queen Macha, a pagan warrior queen, realising the defence value of building a fort on the hill, gave that hill her name..... Ard Macha, Hill of Macha? It is said that she and her descendants ruled Ireland from this place for another 300 years before the seat of power was moved across the Callan River (said to have burst forth during the reign of Tigernmas around 1600 B.C.) to Emania.

Here again, another Macha features greatly as the founder of Emain Macha (Navan). But was that foundation the result of a dispute between three rival kings, Diothorba, Cimbaeth and Aodh Ruadh? This Macha being the daughter of Aodh Ruadh who fought a victorious battle in which Diothorba was killed. This warrior queen, a strong-minded, ambitious woman, then married Cimbaeth thus ensuring that all future disputes were avoided. Having decided to found her royal palace at Emania she lured her enemies into the woods defeating them one by one, then forced them to erect the fort of Emain Macha. Using her brooch-pin Macha marked off the circuit of the Navan Fort and some believe that the name Emain derives from the old Irish word for a neck-brooch, eo-mhuin.

Another tale, however, conjures a more lyrical, mysterious Macha. One night a terrible storm raged around the house of a chieftain, Crunniac. In the morning he awoke to find a beautiful woman outside his house, a woman who could run more swiftly than any horse with her long hair flowing like a mane behind her. Crunniac fell in love with her but, although she loved him too, she would not tell Crunniac her name. As time went on the woman became pregnant and the pair were overjoyed but, as she came close to her time, a message arrived for Crunniac from the king of Ulster to attend a great feast at Emania. Although worried that travelling would be difficult for his wife, Crunniac was afraid to offend the king and so the pair went to the feast.

Caught up in the revelry Crunniac found himself boasting to the king that his wife could outrun any of the king's horses. The king being very proud of the speed of his horses ordered Crunniac's wife to race his fastest horse or see

Crunniac beheaded. The woman had no choice. Angry and warning that a great misfortune would befall them if she was forced to run, she ran the race, "..the horses ran swiftly like a mountain stream but the woman was like an arrow in flight through the air."

At the winning line the woman was the victor and the king stepped forward to demand her name. " Macha ...my name is Macha!" she cried and, as storm clouds gathered and lightning flashed across the sky, she gave birth to twins, then died. But before she died Macha cursed the men of Ulster. "My twins will bring on you a blessing and a curse. The blessing will give you strength and power. The curse will make you weak when you most need to be strong." So from that day the place was called Emain Macha, some believing that the term is taken from old Irish, meaning 'twins of Macha'.

The stories of Navan stirred the blood of pre-Christian boys and girls just the same as they fire the imagination of today's youngsters. It was listening to his father's tales of the Red Branch Knights, the corps of warriors who guarded Ulster during the reign of King Conor MacNessa, that led the young Setanta to walk from Dundalk to

Armagh where he was to become one of Ireland's greatest heroes, Cuchulainn.

Although not welcomed by his uncle, King Conor, the young Setanta soon gained favour when his exceptional prowess at the game of 'hurley' earned him the tutorship of the renowned druid, Cathbad, who agreed to teach him all he knew. Setanta was honoured to be chosen by Cathbad but the druid knowing that Setanta was no ordinary mortal said; "The honour is mine, Setanta. Soon, the whole world will know your name." However, Cathbad was puzzled. He had looked into the stars and read the oracles and could find no mention of Setanta's name and he was worried that perhaps his skills were lessening with old age. But Cathbad soon discovered that it was to be under another name that the boy Setanta would gain world renown.

It seems King Conor was a man of vision as regards public relations. It was his habit to visit, once a year, the craftsmen who serviced Emain Macha believing that the carpenters, smiths, masons and potters were just as important to the survival of the fort as the warriors who protected it. A short time after Setanta had come to Armagh, King Conor and his Red Branch Knights rode out "with a dozen chariots" to visit Culain,

the chief smith of Ulster, at his fort some miles from Emain Macha. Setanta, too engrossed in a game of hurley, (where such was his skill that he played alone against a team of eleven or fifteenother boys) followed later to discover that Culain and his guests had forgotten about Setanta's late arrival and the fort was closed up with Culain's favourite hound, an exceptionally fierce animal, on guard.

Carrying his hurley stick and unaware of any danger, Setanta began to climb the gate only to be knocked to the ground by the snarling hound, the biggest the boy had ever seen, "its teeth were massive, its eyes a dull sulphurous yellow." As lightning flashed, illuminating the hound, Setanta waited for a crack of thunder that would make the hound jump and as the hound leapt towards him, its jaws gaping, he struck his ball with the hurley stick and smashed it into the slavering jaw and right through the back of the dog's skull. The hound was dead before it hit the ground.

Although Conor was relieved to find his nephew unharmed, Culain was angry at the loss of his favourite guard dog, yet amazed when he heard how Setanta had killed it. When Setanta offered himself as a replacement for the guard dog until such time as another hound had reached maturity Culann cried; "This must be the boy Setanta, son of a god and mortal woman......you will be the cú Chulainn, the hound of Culain," and Setanta replied, "Setanta died this night. Henceforth let me be known as Cuchulainn, the Hound of Culain!" And in time he also became known as the Hound of Ulster.

Fortunately for Ulster and Emain Macha, Cuchulainn was not affected by Macha's curse which left the men of Ulster weak when they most needed to be strong. Not having been born in Ulster, Cuchulainn was immune to the curse and he was to prove invaluable as he battled victoriously through the boy troop to take his place with the Red Branch Knights. It was his immunity to Macha's curse which helped the Ulstermen to victory on many occasions especially during the Tain, the cattle raid in which Maeve, Queen of Connaght attempted to steal the great Brown Bull of Cooley.

When Maeve and her husband, Ailill argued over how many riches each of them had brought with them, Ailill topped Maeve's claims with his great White Bull. Enraged, Maeve consulted her wise man and discovered that a man called Daire in Ulster owned an equally great Brown Bull. She was determined to bring that bull to Connaght

and led her armies to attack Ulster. However, Conor and his warriors lay weak from Macha's curse and it fell to Cuchulainn to ward off the attack on his own. For days Cuchulainn battled heroically, his superhuman strength keeping all at bay, including his old friend Ferdia, now one of Maeve's Connaght warriors.

The story goes that Ferdia and Cuchulainn trained together at a military school on what is thought to be the Isle of Skye. Although they played many competitive games the pair never fell out and vowed to remain firm friends forever. However, as they grew to manhood each returned to his native province, Cuchulainn to Ulster and Ferdia to Connaght, but with Maeve's attack on Ulster the two were forced to become enemies.

It is said they fought for four days on the banks of the Boyne, establishing an Irish precedent whereupon brothers have fought brothers and friends have fought friends throughout the centuries. Eventually, "the pair struggled so much in the Boyne that its course was changed and its waters ran red with blood" and on the fourth day Ferdia died. Cuchulainn stayed by Ferdia's body all night and his laments were heard as far away as Scotland.

At last Macha's curse lifted and Conor led his warriors to help Cuchulainn and defeat Maeve's armies but, although in retreat, Maeve drove the Brown Bull of Cooley ahead of her into Connaght. However, when the Brown Bull smelt the White Bull he hurled himself at it and tore the White Bull to shreds before rampaging back to Cooley tearing a deep track through the earth. "When he reached Cooley his heart burst and the blood flowed over the land" and neither Maeve nor Ailill had a bull but, according to the Irish epic, Táin Bó Cuailnge, Aillil and Maeve made peace with Ulster and "for seven years afterward none of their people was killed in Ireland."

From the mound of the Navan Fort which now provides a view of the pinnacles of Armagh's two cathedrals and where children rolled their eggs on Easter Monday, the people of Emain Macha might have watched as Cuchulainn rode triumphantly across those fields, his newly won wife, Emer, by his side. Triumphant because he had overcome all the obstacles that had been put in his way by Emer's father in order to claim the bride that the gods decreed should be his, and because he had been the victor in the terrible battle against Forgal in which Forgal and many warriors were slain. It was from the mound of Navan Fort that Emer watched her husband go

off to his final battle. His mother Deachtaire had gone to see him off and offered him a cup of wine, but as Cuchulainn's lips touched the wine, it turned to blood and his mother, seeing it as a bad sign, tried to persuade him to stay. Did Emer too try to stop him and did she, like women through the centuries, feel the leaden certainty that she would never see her husband again? Or are the thoughts attributed to her in some other stories closer to the truth? "He was fine and strong, handsome, wealthy and loving in his own way. But in truth Cuchulainn really only loved Cuchulainn."

Standing on the mound that rises behind the present-day construction of Emain Macha you might hear the clash of steel on steel as the Red Branch Knights, as legendary as King Arthur's Knights of the Round Table, tested their weaponry in the Craeb Ruadh or hear the laughter of King Conor Mac Nessa as he played fidchill, an ancient Irish board game and thought longingly of Deirdre, the child he had once saved from death only to become the cause of her death. When Deirdre was born the druids foretold her future saying; "….she will grow up to be more beautiful than anyone has ever been. But because of her, many of the heroes of Ulster will die." Conor persuaded the worried warriors not to kill the child saying he would keep her in a safe place until she had grown, then he would marry her.

Sheltered from everyone Deirdre grew into a beautiful woman. One day she saw a calf being killed and watched as a raven drank the blood that had spilled on the snow. That night she dreamed about a warrior "....with hair as black as a raven's wing, lips as red as blood and with skin as white as snow". On wakening she saw Naoise, the warrior of her dreams, and the two fell in love. With Naoise and his brothers, Deirdre fled to Scotland where King Conor could not reach them but Conor sent word that they could return and he would not punish them.

Conor lied. The snow was again on the ground as Naoise and his brothers rode across the plains towards Navan where Conor's warriors waited to kill them, spilling their blood on the white snow. The druid's prophecy had been fulfiled, "Her name is Deirdre - Deirdre of the Sorrows...she will bring sorrow and pain to all the heroes of Ulster".

The fort erected for Queen Macha remained the residence of the ruling monarchs of Ulster for the following six hundred years and its subsequent decline and destruction appear to coincide with the death of Christ and the end of paganism.

Some time around the 1st century B.C., the people of Navan filled the great ritual structure with stones, covered it with sods of earth and set fire to it, possibly as an offering to the gods or perhaps in answer to the call of Christianity. Either way paganism was on the decline.

Legend has it that King Conor Mac Nessa, around 33 A.D., had been seriously wounded by a ball hurled by the Connaught champion. Surgical techniques not being what they are today the king's physician stitched the ball inside the king's brain and told him to take it easy. However, upon hearing of the death of Christ, Conor became so enraged and excited that the ball burst from his head and he died and has since been described as the first Irish martyr and the first pagan in Ireland to have gone to heaven.

The death of King Conor and the decline of paganism saw the beginning of the end of Emain Macha. Around 332 A.D. there began a series of invasions from the south and west of the island which saw the three Collas, nephews of the High King of Tara, the victor's. This resulted in the Ulstermen being confined to the eastern portion of the province and the centre of power moved away from Navan. However, one of the brothers,

Colla Da-Crioch, received the territory of Armagh and it soon reverted to its position of authority.

It is thought that it was the political importance of Armagh within Ireland which attracted St. Patrick to the city in 444 A.D. In the same way as Saints Peter and Paul had gone to Rome, St. Patrick came to Armagh knowing it was the centre of power and therefore the pivot on which his conversion of Ireland turned. At the end of his mission to introduce Christianity to Ireland, Patrick arrived in Armagh where Daire, a descendant of Colla Da-Crioch, gave him the hill of Armagh on which to establish his last and most important church. Around this church, now St. Patrick's (C. of I.) Cathedral, there grew up other religious houses, colleges and schools and the process began which was to make Armagh a great centre of religion and scholars.

Alongside the ghosts of learned and religious men there wander around the capital of Armagh the spirits of the legendary heros and heroins who lived and died here many centuries ago. Perhaps today as the wind whistles through the trees around Navan we can hear Deirdre's wails as she mourns the loss of her lover before dying of a broken heart. Or along the Callan River we might hear, above the rush of water, King Niall's dying screams as the torrent tore him from the bank to a watery grave as he tries to save one of his warriors from drowning after routing the Danes from the city.

Perhaps too the sound of flapping wings as birds head south for winter is really an echo of other wings, those of the Children of Lir, Fionnuala, Aodh, Conn and Fiachra, turned into swans by a wicked stepmother and doomed to spend 300 years on Lough Dervarragh, another 300 on the the Sea of Moyle, and yet another 300 on the wild Western Ocean. The story goes that, seeing the little lough at Tullyvallen, near Keady in County Armagh, the children decided to rest there for a time before continuing their arduous journey to the North Channel (the Sea of Moyle).

Above it all must rise the ghostly whisper of dreams and plans by the men of vision who transformed a collection of mud huts into a 'city of palaces' intermingling with the chant of prayers and low murmur of theological discussion emanating from the spirits of past saints and scholars, who gave Armagh its reputation as ...........City of Light and Learning.

Founded by King James I in 1608 as part of his scheme for the Plantation of Ulster, the original Royal School was situated in Abbey Street on the site of the ruined Church of St. Columba. This building was destroyed in 1642 when the city was sacked by Sir Phelim O'Neill but was re-built in 1657.

When Archbishop Robinson devised a plan to establish a university in Armagh, a larger school was built with a gift of £4000 from the Archbishop and the present Royal School was completed in 1774. In 1849 Archbishop Lord John Beresford enlarged the building and raised it to its present height.

Among its famous old boys is the Hon. Robert Stewart who was at the school in 1777-1781 and afterwards became Lord Castlereagh, Chief Secretary for Ireland in the days of the Union and later Foreign Secretary. James Archibald Hamilton, Dean of Cloyne, was a pupil in 1760 and later became the first astronomer of Armagh Observatory.

One of Lord Castlereagh's school-fellows was Leonard Gillespie, Surgeon and Physician to the Fleet under Admiral Lord Nelson. Dr. Gillespie's diaries are thought to be the only record of life aboard the Victory. In a letter to his sister in 1805 he describes his position as a happy one with a salary of £485 per annum.

Two famous 'barring-outs' or rebellions took place in the Royal School, the first in 1788 when, according to William Blacker of Carrickblacker; "The great cause of the Rebellion was the wish to render a holiday in each week a matter of fixed rule and not a thing discretionary with the masters..." Armed with pistols and ammunition, boys barricaded themselves in a large dormitory and fired shots across the courtyard. When one of these shots almost hit the headmaster's wife, Mrs Carpendale, she wrote "a very affecting letter to the leaders which produced great effect........so ended the affair and with it our chance of an extra vacation."

The story of the second 'barring-out' in 1823 is told by Elizabeth Alexander in 'Lady Anne's Walk' and recounts how some boys put gunpowder behind the fire so that the headmaster, Dr. Guillemard, was blown off his feet. The Doctor threatened to stop all holidays until the "author of the outrage" confessed. War was declared and twenty boys barricaded themselves in a dormitory again shooting at passers-by until the military were called out. Eventually the combination of a truce and the fact that they had run out of water persuaded the boys to surrender .... "The dormitory had fallen."

# The Royal School, Armagh

*With thanks to The Royal School, Armagh*

J. Hynes

Tassagh is just two miles from Keady, where St. Matthew's Parish Church still retains part of the building financed by Primate Robinson in 1775. Keady is believed to have developed in the early part of the 17th century and grew up around a crossroads linking four main garrison towns, Armagh, Monaghan, Mountnorris and Castleblayney. The town became an important bleaching centre for hand-woven linen in the mid 18th century and a market-place for the outlying villages such as Tassagh.

An integral part of Tassagh is the river and the name Tassagh could be derived from the old Irish word for 'waterfall' because of the Callan River running through the area. A contrary view is that the name derives from Assisius, a disciple of St. Patrick, who later became a Bishop and is traditionally believed to have ministered the last rites to St. Patrick.

According to Bassett (1888) the old graveyard at Tassagh was originally intended as a burial place for the secular priests serving in the Culdee Priory in Armagh and it is considered to be one of the oldest graveyards in Ireland. A gold ring containing a 'large emerald in a rich setting' was discovered during excavations in 1824 and a more recent discovery of what appears to be a Lavabo, a washing trough used in medieval monasteries, bears out the belief that a small Priory once stood in Tassagh.

In the 19th century the linen industry flourished around Tassagh and a number of mills were established along the banks of the river. William Kirk's Linen Manufacturers was one such enterprise where linen weaving, bleaching, dyeing and finishing was carried out on 200 power looms in factories in nearby Keady, Annvale, Darkley and in Tassagh. Possibly as a result of the great supply of linen, Keady 'earned a reputation for superiority in tailor-made clothing and shirt manufacture.'

Soon to celebrate its centenary, Tassagh Viaduct still stands on the outskirts of Keady, an impressive testimony to the railway which once ran across it from Armagh to Keady and Castleblayney. The viaduct has been described as the finest piece of engineering on the whole network and consists of eleven arches standing more than 70 feet high and 570 feet long.

# Tassagh Viaduct, Keady

*With thanks to Brian W. Dougan*

Tandragee owes its origins to the St. John family who received a grant of the land during the Plantation of Ulster. The last chieftain, Oghie O'Hanlon, received a grant from Queen Elizabeth for loyal services rendered, however, his heirs later forfeited the land as a result of their participation in the Earl of Tyrone's rebellion (1594 - 1603).

In 1609, when Sir Oliver St. John received the land he rebuilt the O'Hanlon Castle, laid the foundation of the present town of Tandragee for English settlers, and later built the nearby Ballymore Parish Church in 1622.

It is said that Sir Oliver was not wholly convinced of the security of his tenure so, when he built the church, he designed it in such a way as to provide a fortress as well as a place of worship. His fears were well-founded for he was assassinated in 1630 and in 1641 the disinherited O'Hanlon's returned to destroy both the castle and the church.

After the rebellion in 1641, a later owner, Captain St. John, rebuilt the church in 1670, but before carrying out work on the castle he was shot through the head on Drumlyn Hill by followers of the O'Hanlons. The property eventually passed to a Miss Sparrow, whose father Brigadier-General Sparrow had married a daughter of the First Earl of Gosford. When Miss Sparrow inherited the land she set about restoring the church in 1812 and it was during this restoration that a skull with a bullet hole in it was found in the family vault and identified as that of the unfortunate Captain St. John. In 1822 Miss Sparrow married George, Viscount Mandeville, later 6th Duke of Manchester, and Tandragee became the seat of the Montague family.

The present castle was rebuilt by the Duke of Manchester in 1837 and was the Ulster seat of the Dukedom until 1939. During the Second World War American troops were billeted in the Castle and by 1945 it was considered to be in too much disrepair to be used as a dwelling.

In 1955 three Tandragee businessmen converted the castle into a factory for the production of fruit juice and an article in 'Ulster Illustrated' written that year describes how; "In the basement of the castle are the Turkish baths which, together with the extensive cellars, will provide excellent storage for the new fruit juice industry."

# Tandragee Village

*With thanks to Hills Chemist, Tandragee*

St. Patrick's R.C. Cathedral was built as a result of the zeal and vision of a number of bishops but at the same time belongs very much to the people of Armagh, without whose help it might never have been realised. Two Great Armagh Bazaars resulted in money being raised all over the world, firstly to build the Cathedral and then to beautify the interior. The second Great Bazaar raised a world record sum of £30,000 allowing Cardinal Logue to decorate the interior with the mosaic, Italian marble and roof paintings for which it is famous today.

In 1835 Dr. Crolly became the first Archbishop of Armagh to live in the city for three hundred years. After building the seminary, Saint Patrick's College, he embarked on his ambitious project of building a National Cathedral of St. Patrick with the help of local people and priests who organised house-to-house collections throughout the diocese. On St. Patrick's Day 1840 the foundation stone was laid, but by 1847 the collections were needed for famine relief and work came to an end.

When Dr. Dixon became Primate in 1852 he declared Easter Monday as Resumption Monday and work began again on a different design, this time incorporating twin spires rather than the originally planned square tower. The first Great Armagh Bazaar in 1865 resulted in £7,000 being collected from all over Ireland and further afield. A relic of the bazaar is the grandfather clock still standing in the vestry which was donated as a raffle prize but has never been claimed.

It fell to Primate McGettigan, a Donegal man, to complete the work on the exterior of the Cathedral which was dedicated on 24th August 1883. Two marble statues of Primates Crolly and McGettigan, memorials to their work, stand at the top of the steps leading to the Cathedral.

The story goes that a young Armagh woman showing some American visitors around Armagh was asked why there were only eleven figures of the apostles above the front door of the building. "Where's the twelfth apostle?" the American asked expecting to hear about Judas' expulsion. Never stuck for an answer the young woman replied, "That's probably him over there...." pointing to the statue of Primate Crolly!

In 1904 the Cathedral was finally consecrated and the organ, dedicated in 1875, completely rebuilt.

# St. Patrick's Cathedral

*With thanks to Abbott Insurance Brokers*

Over two hundred years ago The Mall was part of the town commons and was surrounded by the 'Horse Course'. However, the bull-baiting and cock-fights which formed part of the post-race entertainment were possibly frowned upon by Archbishop Robinson who put a stop to the activities in 1773 and in 1797 Primate Newcombe handed the ground over to the Sovereign and Burgesses for the use of the towns-people as a public walk.

At one end of The Mall, the Courthouse, designed by Francis Johnston and completed in 1809, succeeds the earlier Assizes House in Market Street. In 1965 there was a complete reconstruction with plasterwork, staircase, balusters and most of the woodwork being replaced. The work was completed in 1971 and just over twenty years later the building was completely destroyed by an IRA bomb.

Some thirty years before the Courthouse was built, the Gaol emerged on the site of the old barracks at the south end of The Mall. It was in the male yard that a scaffold was erected in 1888 for the execution of a man named Thompson and was still standing in 1899 when the Armagh Guardian reported the executions of Kelly and King in the same week.

Kelly was dispatched to his maker with little problem but, when King's turn came to have the rope placed around his neck, one of the attending priests, Father Quinn, noticed that it was not quite 8 o'clock. He insisted that the doomed man be given all the time possible to prepare and "for three terrible minutes, which, it can be imagined, seemed much longer, the party stood there in the grey light, around the trap door, and a more weird scene can hardly be imagined."

The Mall was soon to become a very desirable residential area and the White Walk was built in 1836 to allow those living around The Mall easy access to both sides. When the Boer War Memorial was erected in 1906, the Crimean Cannon, captured during the war with Russia in 1854, was moved to the other side of the White Walk where it still stands.

At one end of the White Walk, Charlemont Place, named to commemorate Francis William, 2nd Earl of Charlemont, was designed by William Murray and was originally intended to house officers of the provincial headquarters. Charlemont Place once housed the nuns of the Sacred Heart Convent who moved there from temporary accommodation in the old Pavilion beside the Courthouse before moving into the Convent built in 1854.

# Charlemont Place, The Mall

*With thanks to Reggie Stinson, Armagh Post Office*

Shrouded in the misty aura of myths and legends that have grown up around the Navan Fort and are today revived and enacted in the award-winning Navan Centre, it is difficult to believe that when Navan's rocks were being formed, Ireland lay on the equator and in its stones lie tales of shark-infested tropical coral reefs.

Archaeological excavations have shown that Navan, or Emain Macha after its renowned founder, Queen Macha, was occupied from the 3rd millennium B.C. but it is famous as the seat of the Kings of Ulster in pre-Christian times and for its mythical and legendary inhabitants, Macha, Deirdre of the Sorrows, King Conor Mac Nessa, Cuchulainn and the Red Branch Knights.

In the 2nd century A.D. Emain Macha (Isamnion) is mentioned by Ptolemy, the ancient Greek geographer; its legendary importance may have persuaded St. Patrick that Ard Macha should be the site for his church; Brian Boru camped at Navan in 1005; King Niall O'Neill built a house there in 1387; and in the middle ages the High King of Ireland, according to law, was expected to be received and feasted at Emain Macha on his circuit of the island. It was also believed that any Ulsterman who did not visit Emain Macha on Hallowe'en (the eve of Samhain) would be driven mad and die the next day!

In more recent times the limestone quarry to the east of the Navan Fort provided the stone for many of the fine buildings for which Armagh is famed but, when archaeological investigations carried out by Mr. Dudley Waterman between 1963 and 1971 revealed that Navan was of major archaeological importance, a group called the Friends of Navan set themselves the task of protecting the area and preventing an extension of the quarry.

Success was theirs in 1987 and the Navan Fort Initiative Group was set up to provide a feasibility study regarding the best future for the monument and its area. In 1993 the Navan Centre, an earth-covered structure depicting the great ritual structure of old, was opened and has since become one of the most important heritage and interpretative centres in Ireland. To quote Brian Musgrave, the Centre's first Director: "May its future be as interesting as its origins."

# Navan Fort

*With thanks to The Navan Centre*

Hamiltonsbawn takes its name from John Hamilton who was granted land there in 1619. As the conditions of the settlement stated that every undertaker of 1,000 acres was bound to erect a strong court or 'bawn', Hamilton built his 'bawn' and settled 26 British families within its surrounds. However, much of the bawn was destroyed by the troops of Sir Phelim O'Neill in 1641, although it is said that one of its stones still survives in the walls of a local 'hostelry'.

The property eventually came into the possession of the Achesons of Markethill and as a result, Hamiltonsbawn was often visited by Dean Swift during his stay with Sir Arthur Acheson in 1729. A particular project for utilising Hamiltonsbawn being considered by Sir Arthur at this time appealed greatly to Swift's sense of humour and he wrote a poem on the subject, entitled; "The Grand Question Debated - whether Hamilton's Bawn should be turned into a barrack or a malt-house."

Although a barracks and not a malt-house was eventually built, old rhymes and jingles collected by T.G.F. Patterson make it appear that Hamiltonsbawn had its share of 'taverns' and 'houses of call' and that the inhabitants spent more time celebrating than working and held a certain disregard for Sunday.

"That in Hamilton's Bawn they're honest and civil,
Believe in God but not in the divil,
They're out in the fields on Sunday,
Digging the praties same as on Monday."

However, Patterson tells us that hunting rabbits and working in the fields was not an unusual occurrence in those days and the reputation for merry-making may have had to do with the hiring fair for which the village was famous and about which it is said that it took the village six months to get back to normal life after each fair.

# Hamiltonsbawn

*With thanks to The Corner Bar*

J. Hynes

The Callan River has been described as "the little known rival to the Boyne" since in 1598 the river formed the background to the famous 'Battle of the Yellow Ford.' The battle was won by the Irish chieftains, O'Neill and O'Donnell, whose armies outnumbered the English army of Bagenal by two to one, and it is said that almost 2,000 men were killed or wounded on the banks of the Callan.

Strangely though, the success of the Irish marked the beginning of the end of native chieftain rule in Ireland and the defeat of Bagenal at the Yellow Ford resulted in the establishment of Ulster as an integral part of the future British Empire.

Many centuries before the Battle of the Yellow Ford, St. Patrick is said to have arrived in Armagh via the old highway, then known as the Green Road, which crossed the Callan at Nursery Road and where, in the early 17th century, a bridge was erected to afford access for the stagecoaches which travelled between Armagh and Dublin. The bridge with its recesses, probably one of the oldest in the area, now forms part of the thoroughfare from Nursery Road to the ring road with St. Catherine's College and Mount St. Catherine's Primary School standing nearby.

A painting of the Old Callan Bridge by the celebrated artist, John Luke, was commissioned by T.G.F. Patterson in 1945 and now hangs in the County Museum on The Mall.

Today the Callan River at that point is often little more than a stream but in 846, when King Niall routed the Danes from Armagh, the river was prone to flooding and was often a fast-running torrent. The story goes that the Danish survivors made for the Callan River, probably hoping to gain refuge at the Navan Fort. A vain hope as they were unable to escape and were annihilated by Niall's army. However a sudden flood, having descended from the mountains around Keady where the Callan has its source, halted the victorious march homewards. When Niall saw one of his warriors in danger of drowning in the treacherous waters he went to his rescue. Unfortunately, as he reached the bank with the rescued man, the land gave way and Niall went to his death in the troubled waters of the Callan. A mound now marks the spot where King Niall III was drowned.

# The Callan River

*With thanks to Annvale Upholstery*

The circular outline of Castle Street follows the inner ring of an ancient hilltop rath which was in occupation as far back as the 5th century. The street, one of the oldest in the city still in continuous use, is said to take its name from the castle which was built there in 1227. T.G.F. Patterson, using the Rentals of the See of Armagh writes that in 1618 Castle Street would have been described as the 'street next to the Friary'. This makes reference to the Culdee Priory which was founded in the 7th century for the secular priests, the Culdees, who served in the Cathedral choir and was situated in Castle Street.

A census of the city made by Primate Robinson in 1770 describes the occupations of some Castle Street folk. William McKee was a school master, Pat Colligan was a labourer and huckster while Nicholas Carson and his wife had a cloth shop and in Chapel Lane, or Mass Lane as it was then known being the site of St. Malachy's Church, the population included five labourers, a butcher and a tailor.

By the late 18th and early 19th centuries the business establishments in Castle Street included 'The Garden of Eden', described in a local newspaper as "one of the most celebrated places of amusement resorted to by the citizens of Armagh." The tavern lived up to its name by providing "arbours, lawns and grottoes" in which the citizens could enjoy their refreshments 'alfresco' and were also entertained by reading the verses and rhymes printed on every available surface.

The verses were the work of the inn-keeper, a character known as 'Paddy Neatcoat' who, being very vain, spent a great deal of time on personal grooming and had an individual way of refusing credit:

> "My liquor's good, my measure's just;
> The times are bad, I give no trust;
> Since man to man has proved unjust,
> Man cannot tell the man to trust."

# Castle Street

*With thanks to City Property Services*

It is said that apples have been grown around Armagh for over 3,000 years. One of the earliest references to the apple being made in the story of Baile, heir to the throne of Ulster, and his love for Aillin, daughter of the King of Leinster. Their parents objected to the match but Baile and Ailinn still managed to communicate and planned to meet. When Baile arrived at the meeting place word reached him that Ailinn was dead and he lay down and died of grief. Ailinn was told that Baile was dead and she too died of a broken heart and tradition has it that an apple tree and a yew tree were planted on the graves.

St. Patrick is said to have planted an apple tree at Caengoba east of the city and the Annals of the Culdees mention that apples were an indulgence allowed the monks during great festivals of the time.

In 1155 the obituary for the head of the Macans, the rulers of an area taking in Loughgall and its famous orchards, praised him for the strong drink made for the use of the clan from apples grown in his orchards. Apple-culture was encouraged by James I during the Plantation of Ulster and, in 1690, King William brought his personal cider maker, Paul Harper, toCounty Armagh to make cider for his armies.

Many local customs have sprung up around the apple. In the last century it was customary to drink a toast to the apple trees, while apples were saved for the last night of January, St. Brigid's Eve, to be made into griddle apple-cake for eating after the making of St. Brigid's crosses.

Apple peelings thrown over the shoulders of boys and girls were said to form the shape of the initials of their future spouse.

Other customs still survive like 'ducking' for apples in a basin of water, using only the mouth to take a bite from the floating fruit or stringing an apple from the ceiling and doing the same without using the hands. These games are still played by children on Hallowe'en night.

A celebration of the apple and apple-growing around Armagh is seen in the Apple Blossom Festival held in May each year.

# Orchard Scene

*With thanks to Wright's Soft Furnishings*

Richhill was formerly known as Legacorry and takes its name from the Richardson family whose castle stands at the top of the main street beside the Parish Church. But the land once belonged to the Sacheverells since Francis Sacheverell in 1610 "received two proportions of 1,000 acres each, called Mullalelish and Legacorry, and elected to reside on the latter portion."

Francis Sacheverell's grand-daughter married Edward Richardson who was MP and High Sheriff for Armagh during Cromwell's time and, through this marriage, the property passed into the hands of the Richardson family, when the name was changed to Richardson's Hill, later shortened to Richhill. By 1664 the present castle had been built.

Edward Richardson's descendant, William Richardson, was also MP for Armagh "when King William camped at Scarvagh" and in 1775 married Dolly Monroe the famous Irish beauty. When, at sixteen years old, Dolly took her place in the social circles of Dublin, it is said her exquisite beauty took the place by storm and "her charms, combined with good looks, cast a complete eclipse over the other Dublin belles."

Goldsmith referred to her beauty in a way that might be considered today as a rather 'back-handed compliment' in 'The Haunch of Venison' when he wrote:

"Of the neck and the breast I had still to depose 'Twas a neck and a breast that might rival Monroe's."

After her marriage to William Richardson, she and her husband spent a lot of their time in Italy where they were said to have a villa and it was believed that the famous Richhill Gates had been transported from Florence. However, an expert on 18th century ironwork has since passed the opinion that they were the work of English or Welsh smiths.

In later years Richhill became a local centre for the linen trade but the market declined when the new road from Armagh to Portadown by-passed the village which is now mainly a residential area.

# Richhill Village

*With thanks to Richhill Insurance*

George Henry Bassett (1888) writes that St. Patrick did not begin to erect the cathedral until 458, three years after his arrival in Armagh. The hill where the cathedral now stands, originally 'Druim-Saileach,' ( hill of sallows) was owned by Daire, a descendant of the Collas, who initially granted Patrick a tract of land on the eastern side of the hill. Excavations in 1979 have shown that Patrick's first church in Armagh was sited in Scotch Street prior to him being granted the high ground.

Over the next 1,200 years the Cathedral was to be burnt, plundered and destroyed many times by the Danes, by Irish and English chieftains, by lightning in 995, by Shane O'Neill and by Sir Phelim O'Neill who in 1641 burned the city as well as the cathedral.

In 1002 Brian Boru, the High King of Ireland, visited the cathedral leaving an endowment of gold and cattle for its upkeep and expressing a wish that he would like to be buried there. After the Battle of Clontarf in 1014 his remains and those of his sons were brought to the cathedral for burial.

During the 17th and 18th centuries successive Archbishops attempted to rebuild and improve the cathedral among these Archbishops Robinson and Beresford. The present building is an 1834 restoration of Archbishop O'Scannail's 13th century church.

During Archbishop Beresford's time in office a full-scale renovation took place not only within the church but also in the cemetery after interments there had been discontinued. A striking picture of the event is painted in a newspaper article at the turn of the century;

"A gruesome sight was presented by the heaps of bones and skulls lying about.....Tom Crow was then sexton....with his fresh, ruddy face, always dressed in a black swallow tailed coat with suitable continuations, but, over and above all stood out in prominent relief of the gloomy clerical-like encasement, a voluminous white neck cloth...."

Tom Crow it is said regarded himself as a "not unimportant member of the Cathedral staff" and was only one of many characters associated with the cathedral. At one time twelve vicars lived on Vicars' Hill, previously the Pound, and other officials lived in Cathedral Close.

# St. Patrick's Cathedral

*With thanks to Abbott Insurance Brokers*

On the east side of The Mall, Beresford Row, named after Lord John George Beresford, Archbishop of Armagh, begins with the Sovereign's House, now the Royal Irish Fusiliers Museum, the first house to be built on The Mall. It was built in 1810 for Arthur Irwin Kelly, the contractor for the Courthouse, and was built using materials left over from the Courthouse. It is said that comment was passed at the time by John Claudius Beresford, uncle of the Archbishop, on "...the coincidence of Mr. Kelly's good fortune." Kelly was the ground landlord for Beresford Row and was created a Burgess in 1805 and later appointed Sovereign.

At one time Beresford Row housed the original Armagh Girls' High School when the school, then known as Richmond High School, moved from Victoria Street and later became amalgamated with Miss Best's Russell Street High School. The school remained there until the Girls' High School (now Armagh City High School) was built at Alexander Road in 1854.

Beresford Row being considered a select quarter of town, it can be imagined how the people there felt about the "cave-like shanty", home of Molly George, that nestled between the Observatory gate and the entrance to the old Pavilion beside the Courthouse. It must certainly have been considered an eyesore by Arthur Irwin Kelly in the Sovereign's House and people like Captain Donellan,

an Inspector of Police married to the daughter of Dr. Carpendale, headmaster of the Royal School who also lived along the Row.

Schoolboys would visit the piece of ground where Molly's shanty squatted, shouting and taunting, but always careful not to get too close as this caused the worthy Molly to run at them hurling threats and abuse, surely uncivilised behaviour in such an up-market area. According to an article in a local newspaper at the turn of the century, "Molly either died in her hovel or her removal from there was effected in some way, but the lairage disappeared at any rate." The ground was levelled and new iron railings put up and today only a lone Lollipop Man patrols the road opposite where Molly's cabin once stood.

# Regimental Museum

*With thanks to J. B. Kingston & Partners*

As with the city of Armagh, Markethill suffered greatly at the hands of Sir Phelim O'Neill in 1641. The castle around which the town was built was completely destroyed as was the Parish Church of Mullabrack, and Bassett (1888) records: "A great deal of suffering inflicted upon the inhabitants of the village."

Acheson's have been associated with Markethill since the first of the line received 1,000 acres from James I and built a stone 'bawn' in which he settled 19 Scottish families and it was in his house within the demesne that Sir Arthur Acheson entertained the celebrated Dean Swift. However, Swift does not appear to have been a particularly welcome guest as it is reported; "...he arrived three days before he was expected and outstayed his welcome by many months......Lady Acheson used all her artifices to get him to leave."

Dean Swift obviously enjoyed his stay in Markethill and once bought a farm from Sir Arthur Acheson which he called Drapiers Field, after the famous Drapier's Letters written under his nom-de-plume. He intended to build a house, however, he later changed his mind but the hill is still called Drapier's Hill.

When the Acheson's were elevated to the peerage in 1806 they became Earls of Gosford and between 1830 and 1839 the present Gosford Castle was built using granite from Mullaghglass quarries near Newry. Again Dean Swift is said to have been a frequent visitor and in later years, during the Second World War, American and British officers warmed themselves in front of the massive marble fireplaces. Drumhead services and fêtes were held on the well-kept lawns, men returning from Dunkirk are said to have rested there and the courtyard often echoed to the sounds of folk songs sung by German prisoners.

In more recent times the castle became the district headquarters of the Forestry Division of the Department of Agriculture and later a hotel. Today its empty windows gaze down upon the oak, ash and elm of its parklands, now Gosford Forest Park.

# Gosford Castle, Markethill

*With thanks to J. D. Hunter & Co*

J. Hynes

The Cope family have been associated with Loughgall since 1611 when Anthony Cope of Hanwell in Oxfordshire was created a baronet and acquired the manors of Derrycreevy and Drumilly from Lord Saye and Sele to whom they had been granted by James I. However, it is likely that he never visited the lands but passed them on to his sons, Richard and Anthony, ancestors of later Copes.

It is said that the Copes were good landlords and they are credited with having introduced apple growing to the area which has since brought worldwide fame to Armagh as the 'Orchard County of Ireland'.

Two famous names are mentioned in the various chronicles of Loughgall, neither of whom would possibly have ever been associated even if they had lived at the same time in history. The first of these is Oliver Plunkett, an Archbishop of Armagh, famed martyr for the Catholic faith and now known as Saint Oliver Plunkett. According to a letter written in 1673 by Captain Walter Cope, Oliver Plunkett was at one time a guest in the Cope mansion. Walter writes: "My acquaintance with this man of gentle birth and much learning has been to me a pleasure to be retained in my memoirs." He later writes about his wife's contemplation on sending their 'dull son' to Plunkett's school in Drogheda but whether he did so is not known.

Over a hundred years later the renowned Dan Winter is mentioned in historical dispatches when in 1795 the Battle of the Diamond took place between Protestant "Pee -o-Day Boys" and Catholic "Defenders". When Dan's house was attacked he and his sons fought desperately to protect their home but the thatch caught fire and they were forced to flee. After the battle, when the dead had been removed and the wounded attended to, the Protestants assembled in the little field in front of Dan Winter's ruined house and vowed to form a society for their future defence and protection. Dan Winter's house became the first embryo Orange Lodge.

# Loughgall Village

*With thanks to W. G. Menary*

The Ensors of Ardress House were descended from an old Warwickshire family, who first came to County Armagh over 200 years ago.

The Ensor brothers, John and George, were both distinguished architects responsible for many of the elegant houses built in Dublin in the 18th century. John is best remembered for the planning and building of Dublin's Rotunda Hospital while George's chief work was the Church of St. John the Evangelist in Dublin.

In 1760 George Ensor married Miss Clarke of Ardress in Clonfeacle Church and some years later the couple took up residence in the Clarke mansion, Ardress House, where George proceeded to remodel the house which had been erected around 1660, the original home having been destroyed in the Civil War of 1641-42. He also built the County Infirmary in Armagh later to become known as the City Hospital.

An outstanding feature of George Ensor's reconstruction of Ardress House still survives in the drawing room richly decorated with ornamental Italian plaster work and boasting a handsome mantelpiece of Italian marble.

George Ensor's eldest son, George, was born in 1769 and educated at the Royal School in Armagh and later at Trinity College, Dublin, after which he was called to the Irish Bar in 1792. He became a well-known political writer and the father-in-law of J.P. Prendergast the historian.

In Armagh County Museum there is a plate and engraving of a painting of George Ensor, an almost complete set of his works, the passports for his Grand Tour of Europe in 1802 and a silver salver presented to him in 1821 in recognition of his efforts to expand the linen business in Armagh and Tyrone.

Over a period of two hundred years the Ensors served as High Sheriffs and Grand Jurors of the county and the last owner of Ardress House, Captain Charles Ensor, was a Deputy Lieutenant for County Armagh. It was this last owner who sold the house to the National Trust and it is said that the auction held there in 1959 attracted antique lovers from all over the province including Dr. McCann, Archbishop of Armagh, who acquired a Welsh dresser for The Palace.

# Ardress House

*With thanks to The Flower Bowl International*

The Sunny Hill, so named because of its ability to bask in the sun at all times of the day, lies to the south of the Palace and looks across the small river to 'Lady Anne's Walk' - not the original walk which is thought to have been near the old Friary, but the second hole of the County Armagh Golf Club course named after the famed sister of Archbishop Robinson.

In her book 'Lady Anne's Walk' Elizabeth Alexander describes the 'Sunny Hill' as seen through the eyes of those unfortunates who would have viewed it from Gallows Hill. She describes it on one corner as a "pleasant slope....peaceful and pastoral" and on the other " a corner of the wide undulating plain of Ulster, reaching to the horizon in Monaghan, bounded in Tyrone by a long line of mountains and stitched here and there with a pale silk thread by the Callan and the distant Blackwater."

Also clearly visible from Sunny Hill are the two huge Sequoia trees, again situated on the golf course and forming a landmark for players on the fifteenth hole which is appropriately named 'Sequoias.' The Sequoias are very tall Californian conifers and were named after the Cherokee indian who is said to have invented a series of characteristics each representing a syllable for his native language.

Lady Anne's ghost may walk the Sunny Hill as it is said to walk the place where her garden once stood and today she might feel that  nothing has changed since visitors now tour the grounds of the Palace in pony and trap with all the atmosphere of bygone days.

# The Sunny Hill

*With thanks to Freeburn Lawnmowers*

Work began on the construction of the Observatory in 1789 and was completed in 1791 and it was to be the Archbishop Robinson's last completed scheme for a public building in Armagh, testimony to his attempt to give the city "... an environment of cultured serenity and good taste."

The Rev. James Archibald Hamilton was appointed as the first Director and a bronze medal was struck by Mossop, the Irish medallist, inscribed: " The Heavens Declare the Glory of God."

At the end of the 18th century the largest telescope in the Observatory was a reflector made and used by William Herschel, famous for his discovery of Uranus in 1781. Scientific discovery was limited and, the general opinion at the time followed the belief of James Ferguson, a scientific writer, that; "It is highly probable that all the planets are inhabited."

In 1821, Lord John George Beresford added another wing and dome to the Observatory but the director at the time, the Rev. W. Davenport, had made few improvements. It seems that the unfortunate man had marital problems and subsequently committed suicide in the Director's study. A later Director, Dreyer noted that Davenport had "died by his own hand, according to Dr. Robinson because his wife was an absolute fiend. Dr. R. had great difficulty in getting her out of the Observatory."

The story that Davenport haunts the Observatory is borne out by a member of staff who, during the sixties, was waiting for the celebrated Patrick Moore, first Director of the Planetarium, to visit. Busy at the telescope he heard footsteps on the stairs and waited expecting to see Moore enter the room. Nothing happened. About half an hour later the astronomer arrived to deny having been there earlier....... the footsteps had to be those of the hapless Davenport!

Later Directors of the Observatory have all left their mark. Dr. Romney Robinson, a writer of poetry at an early age; John Dreyer, a Dane whose grandfather had been a staff officer in Napoleon's army; Rev. William Ellison, a brilliant amateur astronomer; Eric Lindsay, a 'local' boy born near Portadown who rebuilt the Observatory to its present position of eminence in the scientific world; and Mart de Groot, from Holland who not only took the Observatory but also the city to his heart and, although has recently handed over Directorship of the Observatory to Mark Bailie is still very much involved with the city through Armagh Marketing Initiative.

# Armagh Observatory

*With thanks to the Armagh Observatory*

An article in the London Times in 1937 describes the Parish of Tynan as; "situate on the extreme west of the County Armagh, where it is separated from the County Monaghan by a drain...." In ancient times Tynan belonged to the Culdee Priory of Armagh and continued as such for many years with the lands held in charter to the Primate.

The earliest tenant-in-chief mentioned in Irish records is MacIntaggart in 1138 with MacCaseys being the principal tenants in 1455 when a new charter was granted to Patrick MacCasey by the Primate. MacCaseys held the lands until the Plantation of Ulster introduced new settlers among which Robert Cowell, a lieutenant in the service of Queen Elizabeth, became See tenant of Tynan. The tenancy eventually passed to Robert's great granddaughter who married the Rev. John Stronge in 1711 and so began the association of the Stronge family with Tynan until Sir Norman Stronge and his son James were murdered in 1981.

Tynan Abbey was built around the year 1750 on the site of an older mansion and has been added to and improved by successive owners through the centuries. Three 8th century crosses stand in the grounds of the Abbey while another cross in 1834 was repaired and re-erected in the village. It has since been re-sited beside the school.

At one time two flour mills flourished close to Tynan and although veins of coal extended over the whole area they were considered to be too thin for Tynan to have ever become a coal-mining village, but a nearby bog once provided fuel for the villagers.

A rather unflattering rhyme about Tynan was quoted by T.G.F. Patterson in a paper 'County Armagh Rhymes and Jingles' :

> "Sure Middletown's the little dandy,
> But if you drink in Tynan
> It's there they'll pick your pocket handy."

Hardly the case today, if it ever was true, as no public house exists in Tynan where these problems might have occurred.

# Tynan Village

*With thanks to Drs' Gillespie*

During the period of invasions and sackings the Archbishop of Armagh was generally housed outside the area. For a time the Primates had their palaces at Drogheda and Termonfeckin in County Louth and, according to Bassett, there were rooms for the Archbishop in the Culdee Priory in Castle Street. When Dr. Robinson, Lord Rokeby, arrived in Armagh he found the existing primatial residence in English Street to be in very bad condition.

The Primates of Armagh are reported to have kept up great style and dignity, almost regal in wealth and display and Archbishop Robinson used a large part of that wealth for the good of Armagh, including the building of the present Palace in 1770 When the architect, Thomas Cooley, died, the Archbishop's protégé, a local man, Francis Johnston continued his work and is responsible for many of Armagh's fine buildings. It is said that: Archbishop Robinson "....found Armagh in ruins and left it studded with Palaces."

Lord John George Beresford, tried to follow in the footsteps of his predecessor. He raised the Palace from three storeys to four and it seems the Palace and most of the land remained in the ownership of the Beresford family until 1916. He and his sister Lady Anne are immortalised in "Lady Anne's Walk" written by Elizabeth Alexander in 1903.

Elizabeth was the daughter of Primate and Cecil Frances Alexander, the author of the well-known Christmas Carol 'Once in Royal David's City' and the popular hymn 'All Things Bright and Beautiful'. Unfortunately she died before her husband became Archbishop and it fell to Elizabeth to help her father to entertain guests.

The story goes that when Lord and Lady Aberdeen paid an official visit to the Protestant and Catholic Archbishops of Armagh they were reluctant for either Primate to know of the visit to the other one. However, having had lunch with Primate Alexander and his daughter, Elizabeth, they set off to have tea with Cardinal Logue and were amazed to find the same Elizabeth waiting to pour the tea at Ara Coeli, having been asked by the Cardinal to act as hostess for him!

# The Palace

*With thanks to Armagh City and District Council*

After the race-course in Armagh became a public walk in the 18th century, horse races were held at 'Kennedies Plains' near Milford and according to Patterson it was "a very well arranged course with amenities that are missing at Farmacaffly" such as a Stand. However, it was the linen industry of the 19th century which resulted in the village of Milford growing up around the mill built on the River Callan by William McCrum in 1808. The mill was said to be the first in Ulster to spin flax using the dry process.

In 1850 William's son, Robert, changed the spinning mill into a factory for spinning damasks and Bassett reports in 1888, "At present there are 270 looms in full operation ....almost 450 people are constantly employed." Robert McCrum also extended the factory and built the village which gained a reputation for being a 'model of cleanliness and good order'. His own residence, Milford House, later became Manor School, a private school for girls and more recently a special care hospital but both are now closed.

The McCrums appear to have been popular proprietors judging by an article in a local newspaper in 1886 reporting the 'coming of age' festivities organised for Robert McCrum's son, William, attended by William's family and friends and all the workers from the Gillis and Milford factories, 500 in all. The occasion was "availed of by the employees to make a suitable presentation to their young friend and benefactor" and the village of Milford was "beautifully illuminated" with the factory where the entertainment took place "tastefully and artistically decorated." Mr. Robert McCrum, in the speeches which followed, is reported to have said he looked upon them (the workers) as friends and he hoped they looked upon him as a friend. "He concluded amidst loud applause by wishing them every happiness and prosperity in the future."

Today the factory stands idle and the village itself has become more residential with its collection of neat, red-bricked terraced houses looking across the fields where local football and cricket teams are now more readily associated with Milford than the past linen industry.

# Milford Village

*With thanks to Armagh College of Further Education*

J.Hynes.

Behind the Palace the ground rises to Knox's Hill where a 113 foot obelisk was erected by Archbishop Robinson in 1783 as a memorial to the Duke of Northumberland who was instrumental in having the Archbishop transferred from Kildare to Armagh. Concerned also with the lack of employment in the area at the time, the Archbishop saw the building of the obelisk as "a means of honourable employment for the people of Armagh during a time of severe stress."

Archbishop Robinson's successor, Lord John George Beresford, was a man of great personal wealth who owned all of the land surrounding the Palace. However he never married and on his death his cousin, Marcus Gervais Beresford, became Primate in 1862 and his son, George de la Paor Beresford, inherited the land.

When County Armagh Golf Club was formed at a public meeting in the Courthouse in September 1893 it was as a result of a growing demand for the sport among the ranks of the Armagh Archery and Lawn Tennis Club. As a member of the Club, George de la Paor Beresford would have been familiar with the growing interest in the game of golf and he agreed to give part of the land to County Armagh Golf Club. He became the first President of the Club and, in more recent times, when the course became an eighteen hole course, the fifteenth hole was named 'Beresford' in his honour.

The Obelisk now stands guard over the County Armagh Golf course and is a landmark for golfers struggling up the steep slopes of the tenth hole or aiming their tee shot at the thirteenth. The view of the city and surrounding area from the Obelisk has been described by Bassett as "not surpassed by any other at Armagh."

# The Obelisk

*With thanks to Michael Campbell Photography*

The Maxwell family have been associated with Killylea since 1610 when the Rev. Robert Maxwell came from Scotland to be Dean of Armagh. The lands around Killylea then belonged to Trinity College, Dublin and the Rev. Maxwell and his son, Robert, obtained leases of much of the land where they built their home, Elm Park House, in 1625. Robert, Rev. Maxwell's son, became Bishop of Kilmore in 1643 while his other two sons built Fellows Hall and College Hall, the names commemorating the endowment of their land by Trinity College.

In 1832 a site was presented by the Provost and Fellows of Trinity College on which St. Mark's Church was built. It was greatly improved by the Armstrong family who gave the church a bell in 1851 and the tower clock three years later. In 1874 the chancel was added, again at the expense of the Armstrong family, and later three stained glass windows were erected by Colonel Cross of Darton to commemorate Lord John George Beresford, archbishop of Armagh from 1822 to 1864. The Maxwell association with the village died out when a great grandson of the Bishop died in 1891 and the lands were divided between his great nephews, bringing the Armstrong, Close and Strong families into close association.

Bassett in 1888 describes Killylea as "handsomely situated on the side of a hill" and reports that a first-rate fair was held there on the last Friday of every month where "nearly all the farmers make butter and send it to market in rolls."

Patterson mentions the village in one of the old jingles of the 19th century:

"Killylea for drinking tay,
An' Tynan it's the dandy
But Cavanapole's the dirty hole
An' College Hall can bate them all
When it comes till drinking brandy!"

However, an article in a local newspaper in 1908 casts doubt on the theory that 'tay' was the only drink to be had around Killylea when a man "...apparently of the labouring class, came hobbling onto the rere platform at Killylea station, his only attire being a pair of trousers and a shirt." The man had apparently left Loughgilly the previous evening to buy shirts in Markethill. Somewhere between Markethill and Killylea he had met an acquaintance "with whom he had some drinks" and the next he knew was wakening up near Killylea station "in a semi-nude state!" - strong 'tay' around Killylea.

# Killylea Village

*With thanks to T. J. Walker, Armagh*

The Argory and the lands surrounding it have been associated with the McGeough family since the 1740's when Joshua McGeough foreclosed the mortgage on the property from a family named Nicholson.

When Joshua's great grandson, Walter McGeough, inherited the land at Derrycaw and the home-place at Drumsill from his father, he shared his inheritance with his three sisters, but a stipulation of the will decreed that Walter could not live at Drumsill while his sisters were alive. Fortunately for Walter, as his sisters lived to a ripe old age in Drumsill, he decided to build on the lands at Derrycaw and the Argory was designed for him by the brothers Arthur and John Williamson, associates of the famous Armagh architect Francis Johnston, and completed around 1824. It was around this time also that Walter assumed his paternal grandmother's name, Bond, and was afterwards known as Walter McGeough Bond.

Walter's grandmother was Elizabeth Bond, daughter and heir to Walter Bond of Bondville, Co Armagh, after whose family it is said that Banbrook (Bondbrook) Hill in Armagh took its name and a family of whom it is said the French held in high regard. History relates that after the defeat of the French at Carrickfergus in the late 18th century, nearly 120 French prisoners were brought to Charlemont, the home of Viscount Charlemont, commander of the Volunteers. The prisoners were found to be badly in need of boots and, according to John Marshall in his 'History of Charlemont Fort and

Borough'; "...one of the Bonds of Armagh generously provided them with all these necessary articles."

After building the Argory Walter married Mary Joy from Belfast in 1826 but she died in 1829 leaving only one daughter. A later marriage to Anne Smith from Westmeath produced six children, the oldest son, Joshua Walter, inheriting Drumsill while the second son, Ralph Shelton McGeough Bond, later known as Captain Shelton, inherited the Argory.

When Captain Shelton died in 1916 he had no children so both Drumsill and the Argory were inherited by Joshua Walter's son, Walter Adrian McGeough Bond. He sold Drumsill in 1917, later to become a well-known hotel, and his son, Walter Albert Neville MacGeough Bond, gave the house and much of its contents to the National Trust in 1979, in whose care it remains today.

# The Argory

*With thanks to Jacqueline Farrell, Period Doors*

The Palace Stables were built at the same time as The Palace, around 1770 and are constructed from limestone and sandstone which were quarried on the demesne and give the building a pinkish colour. The stables also housed the Archbishop's coachman and other servants and, according to a report in the local newspapers, in 1859 when a fire destroyed a large part of the buildings; "The entire concern was fitted up with all the modern improvements which taste could suggest or a liberal purse supply....".

One of the many servants who occupied the stables over the years is often referred to by Elizabeth Alexander, Primate Alexander's only daughter, as Tummus, (or Thomas) and appears to have been a wily old rascal, given to gossip and story-telling with little time for the day-to-day efforts of his employment: "I found old Tummus scuffling Lady Anne's Walk; that is to say, he was busy looking pensively at the weeds as he leaned on his hoe. He never suddenly pretends to be at work when he is not at work, but always retains the same dignity of carriage."

Before the days when the 'motor car' became an accepted inhabitant of the stables the story is told of how Elizabeth met three lady visitors to Armagh who had arrived by chauffeur-driven car and were dressed in costumes "of the most chic for the automobile." On taking them on a conducted tour of The Palace grounds they were somewhat entertained by the sarcastic Tummus who was not the least impressed by the leader of the group or her manner of dress, saying afterwards; "Do ye know what I'm goin' to tell ye?...As to thon fule wumman, they shud have kep' her in the County Asylum, so they shud, and put her from trapezin' over the country like a play-actor in them jools."

It is reported that the Primates' coachmen were "spendidly dressed, so that when the Primate drove to the Cathedral it was a sight worth looking at.". One of Lord John George Beresford's coachmen later became coachman to Queen Victoria.

# The Palace Stables

*With thanks to Armagh City and District Council*

Cricket was first played on The Mall in 1845 when Mr. Wiltshire, the then proprietor of the Beresford Arms Hotel, leased the central field and opened it to the public. A report in the Armagh Guardian in July 1845 notes that; "...several spirited games of cricket were played thereon." Although cricket is reported to have been played in England as far back as 1550 it seems that its introduction to Armagh was effected due to the quartering of English troops in the city during the late 18th and early 19th centuries and it was not until 1859 that Armagh Cricket Club came into being.

The first meeting of the club was held in the drawing room of the house in Russell Street where Birch's Post Office was installed in 1860. Later it was occupied for many years by the law firm of Monroe and Anderson, now the newly-refurbished premises of solicitor, Brian Dougan. In 1861 Armagh Cricket Club came into possession of its present pitch.

Across the cricket pitch, Mall West is visible through the trees. Nicknamed the Half-Penny side of The Mall because of a certain inferiority to the superior residential area opposite, it turns its back to the view of the two cathedrals enjoyed by Mall East. On this side the First Presbyterian Church raises its spire on the corner of Russell Street. The congregation originally worshipped in a Meeting House close to the Shambles and later in Abbey Street before moving to the present site in 1878.

What has been described as "an enchanting toytown Gospel Hall with a stocky campanile tower" stands on the corner of Jenny's Row which leads onto the main thoroughfare of English Street. Jenny's Row is named after the Rev. Henry Jenny, a rector of Mullabrack from 1708 until 1733, whose residence in English Street was to become known as the Beresford Arms Hotel, now the Bank of Ireland.

It is said that Dean Swift was sometimes Jenny's guest in Armagh and the two were certainly friends as Jenny is mentioned quite often in Swift's works, including a line in the lengthy debate as to whether. "Hamilton's Bawn be turned into a Barrack or a Malt-house" which went as follows; "Swift was so shabby and looked like a ninny, the Captain supposed he was curate to 'Jinny'". The story goes that Swift blamed Jenny for a rather derogatory reply to the verse but innocence was proved and the pair remained friends.

# Cricket on The Mall

*With thanks to Cornett Design Associates*

J. Hynes

The first local infirmary on record in Armagh is the famous "House of Sorrows" a hospital associated with the Red Branch Knights. In Christian times the religious houses in the city, such as the Culdee Priory, provided for the sick and it wasn't until the mid-18th century that a proper hospital was sited in Armagh. This was known as the Charitable Infirmary in Scotch Street where, in 1767, the County Hospital was also housed having been set up as a result of an Act being passed for the provision of county hospitals.

In 1774, the County Infirmary, designed by George Ensor, was built on the site of the home of Thomas Dawson, a Burgess of Armagh during the reign of James I, and after whom Dawson Street was named.

Although the wards were spacious the patients lay in boxes or cupboards which were designed to provide privacy but which probably provided little in the way of comfort or hygiene. Strict rules applied to the behaviour of patients e.g.; Patients spitting upon or otherwise injuring the floor, walls, or boards were liable for discharge and when dismissed were forbidden ever to be received again into the hospital, likewise patients "found guilty of riotous behaviour or indecent language".

On the Surgeon's Roll 1767-1924 only eight names appear. This was due to the fact that two surgeons, Alexander Robinson and Joseph Mansergh Palmer, covered a period of 97 years between them. Robinson (1827 - 1878) was in attendance during the Big Wind of 1839 when the hospital suffered badly and it would have been he who received the authorisation noted in the Minutes of 2nd September 1846 to supply bread to the patients "in consequence of the bad quality of the potatoes." A forecast of the Great Famine to come.

Palmer (1878 - 1924) was in charge of the Infirmary at the time of the Armagh Railway Disaster in 1889, in which eighty people were killed and almost two hundred injured, when an excursion train crashed outside Armagh on 12th June that year.

# The Infirmary

*With thanks to The Queen's University of Belfast*

Kilmore's ancient name of Kilmore-Aedhan is derived from the foundation of a church and small monastery erected in the area by St. Mochtee, the founder of Louth, who dedicated the church to St. Aedan. It has been described as the "site of the first church in Ireland" and was considered an important religious and educational establishment in the days when even the chieftains and other prominent men were unable to read or write and signed important documents with their mark.

It has been said that St. Patrick visited Kilmore on his way to Armagh in 455 A.D. and "was hospitably entertained by these primitive Christians". If this is true, it would give Kilmore a certain priority over the City of Armagh.

Like Markethill and Hamiltonsbawn, Kilmore saw strange new communities settle in the area during the Plantation of Ulster and it seems the old church was replaced around 1620 with a larger, newer structure as an extract from a report dated 1622 states: "Rector resident, a fayre church now built, a parsonage house now built in ye old 'Glebe', with slates, barn and an orchard planted which hath cost £200." This building was replaced in 1814 but the old tower with its nine feet thick walls remained.

Again, like Markethill and Hamiltonsbawn, Kilmore claims association with Dean Swift although the relationship does not appear to be a happy one. The story goes that Swift had arranged to preach at Kilmore Church and after robing in the vestry awaited the ringing of the bell to indicate the time when he should proceed to the sanctuary. Time passed and no bell was rung so Swift impatiently inquired of the verger the reason for holding up the service. The bell-ringer replied that, "The Richardson coach has not yet topped the hill," the service awaiting the arrival of the Richardson's of Richhill. In a temper, Dean Swift stormed from the church saying: "If the bell of Kilmore Church is to hang on the wheels of the Richardson carriage I do not preach here!"

# Kilmore Village

*With thanks to Glass Brothers*

The City of Armagh was already known as an ancient market town in 1467 when the then Archbishop received confirmation of an existing charter from Edward IV. Through the centuries markets were held in what was then known as Market Place which contained the early medieval Market Cross, (part of which is preserved in St. Patrick's Cathedral), the old Sessions House and Prison and the Market House.

In the 17th century the majority of criminals in the Market Street prison, which stood where Whittsitt's now stands, consisted of thieves. But the theft of a firkin of butter was treated in the same way as the theft of horses, pigs, sheep and oxen and the death penalty was the accepted sentence. Prisoners were taken "down the nine steps" to underground cells in McCrum's Court before being taken up Market Street, along Castle Street and down Irish Street to Gallows Hill, then part of the Demesne, to be hanged. Their heads would then be displayed on the wall of the prison, their dead eyes gazing down on the stallholders and customers of the market.

Many famous outlaws also met their fate in this way, the most famous being possibly Redmond O'Hanlon, whose exploits attracted Sir Walter Scott so much that he intended to write about him in an historical novel. However, he never carried out his intention and the material he had collected has been lost. O'Hanlon appears to have been an Armachian Robin Hood, well-liked by the poor and the subject of many folk stories. One of these relates how O'Hanlon took exception to a man who robbed a pedlar in his name. In retribution O'Hanlon deliberately delivered the man to Armagh Jail knowing that, according to T.G.F. Patterson; "...he would swing on Gallows Hill and his head later decorate the sessions house."

The Armagh Guardian of 1898 reports that; " One of the last public executions was that of a woman, who it was said, ....... picked her steps daintily across the dirty street on her last walk to the prison..." Her crime was aiding the murder of her much-older husband by a young lover "to whom she had taken a fancy."

# Market Street

*With thanks to Armagh City and District Council*

Traditionally the main market in Armagh was held in Market Street with other markets having their own speciality. In 1855 the Flax Market began at Irish Street. The Linenhall Market in Dobbin Street, set up by Leonard Dobbin, a pioneer of town planning in Armagh, later became the Egg and Butter Market.

A market for live pigs was held in Barrack Street and at the Shambles' was the cornmarket specialising in grain, seed, hay, straw and pork. The Shambles Market with its clock tower was built for Archbishop Beresford in 1827 on what was then known as Mill Street and appears to have been quite a dangerous place in the early 19th century. An Armagh newspaper of 1882 relates how James Black, a well-known artist who painted the signboards for the local taverns, "...came to an untimely end being murdered at the Shambles on his way home" in 1829. However, racial discrimination was obviously not a fault as the newspaper reports that the next unfortunate victim to be murdered there in 1835 happened to be a man called White!

Around the corner from the Shambles Market, in lower English Street, the Assembly Rooms were replaced in 1794 by the Tontine Rooms which consisted of "tea, card and coffee rooms of elegant design", a ballroom and a suite of apartments in one of which a News Room was established. The Tontine Rooms also served as Armagh's theatre and many well-known entertainers of the past including Percy French and the renowned General Tom Thumb performed to packed houses.

In 1908 the Tontine Building was demolished and the City Hall erected in its place. Unfortunately it was destroyed by an IRA bomb in 1972 and never rebuilt.

Across the road is the Charlemont Arms Hotel, named after the famous Volunteer Earl of Charlemont. Once known as the Caulfield Arms, when James Caulfield, the 4th Viscount, was created earl in 1763, the name was changed so that travellers through the city might be suitably impressed.

A hotel that remains fondly in living memory is the Beresford Arms Hotel at the top of Jenny's Row. Originally the 'King's Head' it later became 'the Molyneux Arms' then the 'King's Arms' and later the 'Royal Hibernian'. By 1844 the hotel had been renamed 'The Beresford Arms' and was the headquarters for Thackeray on his visits to the city.

# View over Armagh

*With thanks to the Forster Family, Charlemont Arms Hotel*

# Armagh, City of Light and Learning

The name Ard Macha can be translated as 'the Hill of Macha' after the great Queen Macha who ruled there in pre-Christian times, or simply 'the high place or field' as translated by Ussher, Ware and Harris. Ard Macha has metamorphosed through 'Armachan' used by King Henry VIII in 1542, 'Ardmagh' by King James I when he incorporated the inhabitants into a borough, to 'Armagh' as it is known today.

Armagh is reputed to have been a hilltop settlement as far back as 3,000 B.C. and was clearly a site of great importance as the regal seat of the Kings of Ultonia through pre-Christian times. Although the centre of power moved across the Callan River to Emain Macha for a number of centuries, the hilltop site regained its importance when the Kings of Ultonia were defeated in 332 A.D. Three brothers, Colla Uais, Colla Da Crioch and Colla Mean, defeated Fergus, the last of the Ultonian Kings, and drove the Ulstermen into the north-eastern part of the island, whereupon Colla Da Crioch received the territory of Armagh and it reverted to its original superiority. These Colla brothers were to be the predecessors of the most powerful families in Ulster, the O'Neills, the MacDonnells of Antrim, the MacMahons, MacGuires of Fermanagh and the O'Hanlons.

Tradition has it that over a century later one of the new line of chieftains, Daire, a descendant of Colla Da Crioch, was approached by a man called Patrick who wanted to build a church on the hill known as Druimsailech, the hill of sallows, within the ancient entrenched enclosure. Daire refused but allowed Patrick to build his church on another site to the east of the city and the church of Na Ferta came into being where St. Patrick's Fold stands today.

Excavations in the 1970's and 80's provided material evidence of an early Christian site there, and the discovery of an underlying spring bears out a report in the Book of the Angel, a 7th century text in the Book of Armagh, that, "Saint Patrick was baptising persons at the spring which is hard by the eastern side of the city....."

Later, Daire having embraced Christianity, Patrick was granted the hilltop site where he was to build his second church and there grew up around it other churches, schools and habitation. According to tradition, when Patrick climbed to the top of the hill, he found a doe with its fawn. His companions wanted to catch the fawn and kill it but Patrick forbade them to do so and, instead, lifted the fawn and carried it to the top of another hill, its mother following. This hill to the north of Druimsailech is believed to be the site on which St. Patrick's Roman Catholic Cathedral now stands.

In those early Christian times Armagh was divided into 'trians' or wards with the Trian Mor including the present Irish Street area and the western part of the town, the Trian Masain occupying the area now known as Scotch Street, Market Street and part of Thomas Street and the Trian Saxon now Abbey Street and English Street. The Abbey of Saints Peter and Paul, which gave the street its name, was attached to the school established by St. Patrick and students from every Christian country soon flocked to Armagh where Bassett (1888) reports that, "...its graduates in theology were preferred to all others." At one time 7,000 students were studying in Armagh, many of whom were English thus giving their name to the quarter in which they lived, and anyone who had

not studied in Armagh was not allowed to teach or lecture on theology.

Although the cathedral was built from stone, the rest of the town was constructed of wood and a number of accidental fires reduced the city to ashes during the 7th and 8th centuries. But it was from external forces that Armagh was in most danger throughout the 9th and 10th centuries.

The Danes were responsible for much destruction from 836 A.D. onwards when Turgesius captured the city, plundering the churches and driving the Bishop, priests and students out. Although the people returned to their ruined homes and managed to live in peace for a number of years, the marauding Danes returned time after time, rasing the city to the ground each time and plundering everything of value. Bassett writes, "They destroyed everything of value in the way of records and carried away relics of antiquity in the precious metals, the value of which in our day would be beyond the power of estimation."

The Danes however did not have everything their own way when they came up against the might of the armies of King Niall who routed them from Armagh during the 9th century and later King Brian Boru defeated the Danes at the Battle of Clontarf in 1014.

According to tradition, Brian Boru, the High King of Ireland, visited the Cathedral in Armagh in 1002 leaving an endowment of gold and cattle for its upkeep and expressing a wish that he would like to be buried there. The writings of one Curne O'Lynn possibly around the beginning of the 19th century, describe the wake after the burial of Brian Boru "...the clargy had a quare spree to thimselves, so they had, as i'm a sinner, they waked the bodies for 12 nights, radin salms, and some say they smoked Dane's pipes and drank whiskey....!" Although the veracity of this account is unlikely to be proven, it is a matter of record that, after the Battle of Clontarf in 1014, Brian Boru's remains and those of his son and nephew were brought to the Cathedral for burial.

Having survived the Viking invasions, the city had just begun to revive when the Anglo-Norman invasion of Ulster began with the arrival of Sir John de Courcy in 1179 and Armagh was almost completely destroyed. Sir John's successor, Sir Hugh de Lacy, continued the destruction and history records that between 1184 and 1217 the city was sacked at least nine times.

However, Armagh still retained its reputation as a seat of learning and it was towards the end of the 11th century that St. Malachy was born in Armagh, a "great and pious scholar" and a man who was to become a leading figure in 12th century ecclesiastical reform. Malachy was the last native of Armagh to occupy the See of Patrick until the late Cardinal O'Fiaich became Primate in the 1970's and is described as a "brilliant lamp" in the Annals of the Four Masters. A plaque in Ogle Street marks St. Malachy's birthplace and, in 1750, a chapel in what is now known as Chapel Lane was dedicated to him, with the new chapel in Irish Street later becoming the present St. Malachy's chapel.

Another great scholar who left a constructive mark on medieval Armagh was Archbishop O'Scannail who rebuilt the Cathedral and introduced the Franciscan Friars to Armagh. In 1264 he built a Friary for them, considered to be the longest Friary in Ireland, and the Friars played a large part in the religious life in Armagh for the next three hundred years. As the Friary was built outside the entrenchment surrounding the cathedral and the main part of the city, a deep trench and a strong rampart acted as a defence for the Friary, but no trace of this earthwork survives. It is said that stones from the Friary were used to build a wall around Lady Anne's garden in The Palace Demesne during the 19th century and today very little is left of the original building.

The 14th and 15th centuries were relatively peaceful times for Armagh, although still punctuated by outbreaks of trouble and tragedy. A new class of society began to form in Ulster in which merchants prospered, but there is little known about the business life of Armagh during that time as ecclesiastical affairs still took priority. However, although a market is mentioned as far back as 1031, it is known that Edward IV granted a charter to Archbishop Bole in 1467 whereby Armagh was granted a weekly market and the Archbishop the feudal rights of that time.

Trouble again flared with the Reformation and the Dissolution of the Monasteries in 1536 which destroyed the educational structure of Armagh. Shane O'Neill's armies are said to have "kept the people of Armagh in a constant state of misery" and when the cathedral was used as a storehouse by Queen Elizabeth's troops, O'Neill destroyed the cathedral and the city so that it might not give shelter to his enemies. Although the English tried to appease the O'Neills by making Con, father of Shane, earl of Tyrone in 1542, Shane refused to accept the title and some years later tried to

persuade Charles IX, King of France, to send 6,000 soldiers to help him drive the English out of Ireland. However, by then he had lost much of his power among the local people and, during a visit to his Scottish allies, he was murdered in 1567.

It is interesting to note that, during this period of constant unrest in a city renowned for its scholastic output that elsewhere in the world the Gutenberg press, an invention that was to revolutionise printing and communication worldwide, was already having a lasting effect on Europe,. At the same time Copernicus, the astronomer, was putting forward his theory that the Earth, like the other planets, revolved around the Sun, not as Ptolemy's theory suggested that the Earth was the centre of the Universe.

Of course, for the people of Armagh, the city and its troubles were still very much the centre of their universe and, according to Bassett, Hugh Roe O'Neill, Earl of Tyrone "made the period of his rebellion, 1594 - 1603, an eventful one" for them. The story goes that O'Neill was a favourite of the Queen but he made use of his time at Court by learning the English system of military organisation and, on his return home, instructed his followers in tactics and the making of bullets from sheet lead. The result of his learning was the famous Battle of the Yellow Ford in 1598 in which O'Neill's armies, supported by those of the O'Donnell, slayed the English commander Sir Henry Bagnall and defeated his army. In 1607, O'Neill and O'Donnell attempted to organise a new rising but the attempt failed and they fled to the continent where they are said to have died in Rome some years later.

Following the Flight of the Earls, Armagh and the surrounding area was "in a pitiful state" and King James I attempted to bring some order to the Ulster countryside by bringing in Scottish and English settlers to replace the native landowners. These settlers were mainly given the lands originally owned by O'Neills and O'Donnells and in 1608 the Plantation of Ulster began which saw the settlers building fortified houses and 'bawns' to protect themselves and their tenants.

Around this time, Armagh still retaining its charter as a market town, James I granted the city a further Charter by which it became a Borough and the government of the city was placed in the hands of a Sovereign and twelve Burgesses, the Sovereign to be elected from among the Burgesses on 24th June each year.

The Tuesday market was confirmed to Archbishop Hampton and his successors in 1614 and two fairs were allowed to be held, one on 17th March, the other on 1st August. According to T.G.F. Patterson, "The patent invested certain curious powers in the Archbishop such as causing troublesome women to be placed in trebuckets or cucking-stools, confining fraudulent bakers in pillories and the plunging of brewers who made bad ale into well-filled dung-carts." However, Stuart records that, "These punishments are not required in this city. There have been but four notorious scolds in Armagh during the last century. One of these, a Mrs King, poisoned her husband, and her eloquence was stopped by the hangman...!" While this was happening in Armagh, in France one of the first successful professional women writers, Marie le Jars de Gournay, was publishing a controversial book on sexual equality.

Although James I's Plantation of Ulster resulted in many problems for the area, a more positive aspect of his reign was the setting aside of lands for educational purposes and the founding and endowement of the Royal Schools of Ulster in 1608. Lands in Armagh and Dungannon were to be leased by appointed headmasters and schools built.

# Light & Learning

By 1614 there appears to have been a delay in the building of the schools but on a subsequent order from King James the Royal School of Armagh was quickly built on the site of the Church of St. Columba in Abbey Street, reasserting Armagh as a seat of learning.

Trouble broke out again in 1641, when the Irish under Sir Phelim O'Neill attempted to regain their lost lands and Armagh once again became a battleground. Sir Phelim was driven out but in the course of the campaign the Cathedral was burned once more and the castles at Tandragee and Markethill destroyed. When Owen Roe O'Neill succeeded Sir Phelim his army defeated General Monroe at the Battle of Benburb in 1646, however, Owen Roe is said to have died of poisoning in 1649 and Sir Phelim, taking up arms again after his successor's death, later surrendered and was hanged in Dublin.

Many planters were killed during the Civil War and their houses destroyed, but after the defeat of the Irish they returned to reclaim their lands and start over again. Among these settlers were the Copes of Loughgall who are credited with having introduced apple-growing to the Armagh area. Although the apple had been grown in the area for many centuries, it was not until the Plantation of Ulster that a systematic method of planting fruit trees was undertaken and clauses were inserted in leases requiring tenants to plant as many fruit trees as their acreage allowed. Although many of these orchards would have been destroyed during the Civil War, records show that cider was manufactured during the period of the Restoration and in the war between James II and William, Prince of Orange, it was being made in some quantity for the use of William's army, William having brought his personal cider-maker to county Armagh in order to supervise its manufacture.

Whether this consumption of cider, as T.G.F. Patterson records, "...that much cider was consumed by his (William's) soldiers in the spring of 1690...." had any bearing on the result of the ensuing battle or not, suffice it to say that, with William's victory at the Battle of the Boyne and the defeat of James II, the end of the Williamite Wars brought a welcome period of peace to Armagh.

Although ale was the usual tipple for kings and peasants alike, (even St. Patrick had his own brewer) by the end of the 17th century, cider had become equally popular and was served in the many licensed premises known as 'Houses of Call' where food and lodging were also provided. According to Patterson, "...our ancestors took an intelligent interest in the consumption of liguor....they drank when they had thirsts so that they might be cured of them, and also when not thirsty in case such a danger should overtake them." A philosophy of prevention being better than cure to which many still subscribe.

Many 'Houses of Call' are recorded at this time including possibly the oldest surviving premises 'the Hole in the Wall' which adjoined the old prison in McCrum's Court. An old hostelry in Abbey Street is said to have housed King James on his way to Derry in 1689 and later was the quarters of the Duke of Schomberg, King William's famous general. In 1703 the two chief inns in the town were the 'King's Arms' and the 'Sign of the Swan' both in Market Street.

At this time The Mall was a commons, a marshy piece of ground around which horse races were run. Records show that the sport was encouraged by the Sovereign and Burgesses who, in 1731, subscribed towards a prize for the winner and fixed prices for stands and booths on the course. However, the bull-baiting and cock-fighting that accompanied the races was often the scene of much drunkenness and rowdiness, behaviour

which was not very well tolerated. Noisy or abusive drunks in those days did penance in the stocks and in 1738 records show that a "sufficient pair of new stocks" was made in an attempt to keep revellers subdued.

Although a certain peace reigned in the area for a time, the Williamite Wars had resulted in Anglican Protestants having the upper hand and between 1695 and 1727 a series of laws passed by the Irish Parliament known as the 'Penal Laws' meant that a number of restrictions were placed on non-Anglican denominations, especially Catholics and Presbyterians, who were not allowed to hold any office of state, stand for Parliament or even buy land.

Many people, dispossessed of their lands, unable to find work, turned to crime, and outlaws and robbers continued to strike fear into the hearts of the local populace. The old prison, where Whitsitt's now stands, echoed to the cries of condemned men and women as they awaited their turn to take that last walk along Castle Street and Irish Street to Gallows Hill. One of the customs of the time was for a mob armed with staves and clubs to form themselves into companies and escort the condemned prisoner to Gallows Hill, "rattling their staves in concert as they marched."

# Light & Learning

However, entertaining as this activity was, on some occasions the crowd allowed their interest to be deflected as on the day in 1721 when the set of six bells presented by Primate Hampton to the Cathedral arrived in the city. History records that; "...coming on to the hour when an unfortunate wretch was to be hanged a crowd had assembled to watch the execution.......a messenger ran to tell the people the bells were coming.....the people instantly forgot all about the execution and ran to escort the bells to the Old Church and give as much help as they required in pulling the great loads up the hills." On this occasion the execution was carried out with no-one but the Sheriff, the gaoler and, of course, the condemned man present.

Religion has always been an important aspect of Armagh life. The mid-18th century saw churches being built for a variety of denominations. In 1722 a Presbyterian Church was built in Abbey Street and Bassett maintains that materials from the ruins of the Abbey of Saints Peter and Paul were used in its construction. It was later remodelled in 1880 before which another two Presbyterian Churches were built on the eastern side of The Mall.

In 1750 ground belonging to the Annesley family off Castle Street was leased by the Catholics of the town and a new chapel dedicated to St. Malachy was built, according to Stuart, "..near the spot where Temple Brigid formerly stood." Later the land was purchased by Leonard Dobbin, a local Member of Parliament who was to be a pioneer of town planning in Armagh, and he granted a lease for 999 years at 5d. per annum. He was presented with a silver cup valued at £50 in gratitude for his generosity.

Mass Lane, later known as Chapel Lane, connects Castle Street with Ogle Street. Both Thomas Street and Ogle Street were named in 1759 to perpetuate the name of a Sovereign of the town, Thomas Ogle, whose mill for cutting and polishing marble stood within the present Demesne and is described by Elizabeth Alexander as providing the great slabs of marble "which pave the streets of the City of St. Patrick."

Methodism is said to have received an impetus in Armagh in 1767 when John Wesley arrived in the city to preach to his followers. However, the story goes that on beginning his sermon at the Market House on one occasion he was interrupted by the Sovereign and forbidden to preach. Fortunately a wealthy merchant named

William McGeough invited Wesley to preach outside his house in Abbey Street but after several visits to Armagh "the house was found insufficient to contain half of the congregation which had assembled to hear his discourse." In 1786 a meeting-house was built by the Methodist Society near the McGeough house and was later remodelled in 1888.

It was during this period that Richard Robinson became Archbishop of Armagh in 1765. According to history, at that time Armagh was in a sorry state having suffered greatly from various wars over the past two hundred years and it is said that only three houses in the town had slated roofs. The Archbishop's house was in English Street but, it also being in bad repair, Primate Robinson lived at Richhill Castle while repair work was being carried out.

In 1769 an Act of Parliament set aside 300 acres of Church of Ireland property as a Demesne for the Archbishop, and on this land Primate Robinson began the building of his Palace which was completed in 1770. However, this was only to be the first of many impressive buildings erected by Primate Robinson. Within less than thirty years Armagh was to be transformed from a collection of mud-huts into a Georgian city worthy of its ecclesiastical eminence thanks to the munificence and industry of Archbishop Robinson.

During those years the Primate was also responsible for the building of the Public Library in 1771 to which he endowed his own collection consisting of works in theology, science, travel and archaeology. The Library also holds rare manuscripts such as the dictated trance visions of St. Catherine of Sienna and Johnathan Swift's annotated versions of the famous "Gulliver's Travels". In 1774 the Royal School, commonly known then as 'the Eton of Ireland', was erected on its new site on College Hill and, in that same year, the County Infirmary was built to the design of George Ensor. Many other buildings were to be erected by Archbishop Robinson including the Observatory, the Courthouse, the Prison and The Palace Chapel and he was responsible for extending the row of houses built by Archbishop Boulter for the widows of clergy which was to become known as Vicars' Hill, as well as building and improving a number of other houses in English and Scotch Streets.

But besides the erection of impressive buildings other improvements were the legacy of Primate Robinson to the City of Armagh during the late

# Light & Learning

18th century, including, as Bassett writes, improvements under ground as well as over ground and "in his time a good beginning was made in the matter of sewerage," work which he initiated being carried on in later years at the expense of property owners in various districts.

Street lighting was also an amenity that originated during the Primate's time with the original lighting consisting of oil lamps in 1776, later lit by gas with the establishment of the Gas Works, a limited liability company set up in Gas Lane, and by 1887 it is recorded that the lighting and maintenance of 247 gas lamps were costing £198-16s a year.

The mid-18th century saw Armagh's first local newspaper being published by William Dickie who was later admitted a Freeman of The City in 1740. By 1787 it seems Armagh was the proud possessor of a fire-engine, a much needed piece of equipment considering the damage fire had done to the city over the centuries.

It was also at the end of the 18th century that a water supply came into existence in Armagh when Lady Primrose, after whom Primrose Hill was named, left a legacy of £1,000 to be applied to a "useful purpose". The trustees of her will bought Lowry's Lake from which water was piped to supply the city. Lady Primrose was the daughter of Charles Drelincourt, Dean and Rector of Armagh in 1691, whose widow endowed a school for the "maintenance of twenty boys and twenty girls" which became Drelincourt School. Unfortunately no trace of Gas Lane, Primrose Hill or Drelincourt School exists today.

By 1782, with the easing of the Penal Laws, Catholics were once again on an equal footing with their Protestant neighbours and were allowed to purchase and hold leases on land. This worried many Protestants however and led to outbreaks of violence in the countryside between the Protestant 'Peep o' Day Boys' and the Catholic 'Defenders', small groups of opposing factions who burned each others homes and fought a number of battles. In 1795 during one of these confrontations, the Battle of the Diamond at Loughgall, Dan Winter's house was burned and he and his sons forced to flee. Afterwards the Protestants gathered in a small field in front of the Winter house and formed what was to be the first Orange Lodge.

Meanwhile, in Dublin, a young Protestant lawyer, Theobald Wolfe Tone was forming a new organisation, The Society of United Irishmen, whose aim was "to unite the whole people of Ireland, to abolish the memory of past dissensions and to substitute the common name of Irishmen in place of the denominations of Protestant, Catholic and Dissenter…" The organisation gained support among Presbyterians in Ulster, although few Catholics joined, and Bassett writes that many "disaffected inhabitants of Armagh" enrolled for service during the Rebellion of the United Irishmen. However, although the 1798 Rebellion was a failure, the events of the late 1700's were to have a lasting effect on Irish history and continue to affect politics today.

Meanwhile life continued in Armagh and the local populace appears to have combined industry with politics. Stuart records that the land around Armagh "abounded with lakes, marshes and unclaimed bogs" and at the beginning of the 18th century a small lake, Lake Lappan, which was said to contain many eels, could be found at the bottom of Market Street. Until 1787 another lake covered much of the land in the Demesne and was used as a feeder for the stream used by Thomas Ogle's marbling mill, and a number of stagnant pools were to be found on Barrack Street Commons. However, during the 18th century, it seems these lakes and swamps were drained leaving a "pure and healthy" atmosphere within the city. It is to this atmosphere, combined with a flourishing linen industry, that Stuart credits an apparent improvement in the demeanour and attitude of the town's inhabitants. "The people are more habituated to habits of industry and less addicted to drunkenness than formerly - an effect partly due to the flourishing state of the linen manufacture and partly to the high price of spiritous liquors."!

Linen was to become an important industry in Armagh. Even as far back as the 16th century linen appeared to be produced in great abundance and it is said the local gentry were wearing shirts containing thirteen to fourteen yards of the material! In the late 17th century, the linen trade in Ireland was encouraged at the expense of the woollen industry and the inventions of the 'spinning jenny' by Hargreaves and a water-powered loom by Arkwright around 1769 were to transform working conditions and productivity in the textile industry in general.

The increase in industriousness noted by Stuart was also seen in the variety of markets which sprang up around the city. Although Armagh markets came into their own during the 17th century, it was towards the end of the 18th century that other markets besides the main one were established when the inhabitants of Market Street petitioned the Sovereign and Burgesses to move the market to a more convenient site. The market was transferred to the northern end of The Mall and later became the horse and pig market in Barrack Street.

In the early 19th century, the Shambles Market was built by Archbishop Beresford as a meat market where the butchers of the town congregated and in 1857 it was extended and improved to include the Hide Market and later a market for Irish-grown hay, grass and flax seed. In 1855 the Flax Market was established in Irish Street to allow for a clearer thoroughfare in the centre of the city and the Egg and Poultry Market which had been housed in the Linen Hall was moved to premises in Dobbin Street to make room for the Butter Market which was rapidly increasing at that time.

Leonard Dobbin, considered to be a pioneer of town planning, was responsible for the building of the Linen Hall where the linen merchants of the time displayed their wares. He also built Dobbin Street and his Johnston-designed residence on the site of St. Patrick's first church in the Na Ferta area later became the Bank of Ireland and is now St. Patrick's Fold. Dobbin's Walks, a park donated

to the city by Leonard Dobbin, later became known as Dobbin's Folly, and was described as a place of "rural and pleasant walks" and a "charming retreat" which attracted men of "contemplative and tranquil minds, who love to listen to the clack of mills ...and who hear with delight the murmur of descending waters and the choral song of birds." The mills mentioned might have included the many flour-mills at places such as Lurgyvallen, Umgola and Ballynahonebeg producing the flour which led Stuart to assert that, "There is no part of Ireland in which better bread is made than in Armagh."

Patterson writes that tanning, turf-cutting, apple-cultivation and the manufacture of linen were the main industries around Armagh for some centuries but it was the linen industry which flourished at the beginning of the 19th century with the Callan River as its focal point.

The Callan is considered to have been instrumental in the rise of the linen industry around Armagh as it was along its banks that the 'Linen Lords' built their factories, beetling mills and scutch mills. Villages and towns such as Milford, Tassagh, Bessbrook and Keady grew up around the mills, and names like William Kirk and Robert McCrum became an integral part of the history of the linen trade in the area.

Bassett records that during the 19th century "two navigable water-ways facilitate the carrying trade of the county" one of which was the Newry Canal and the other the Ulster Canal, the latter being used extensively by the merchants of Armagh loading their merchandise at Blackwatertown. The advent of the railway provided a further means for merchants to transport their goods but it also led to a decline in local fairs and markets and the smaller industries like brewing and rope-making. Although it was not until 1848 that the Armagh line was opened, Patterson records the first printed reference to the railway as being in 1804 when "...an iron road had been talked about but no decision had been made."

The Armagh-Newry line which was linked up in 1865 has gone down in history as the scene of Ireland's worst railway disaster. In 1889 eighty people were killed and almost two hundred injured when an excursion train crashed on the outskirts of Armagh. However, although a tragic event, the disaster produced a much-needed Act which enforced automatic braking, block signalling and the interlocking of all signals making for safer rail journeys in the future. Although some railways did take safety precautions, these were not compulsory until the Regulation of Railways Act was passed in 1889 as a direct result of the Armagh Railway Disaster. Unfortunately Armagh is no longer connected to the rest of the province by rail as the line was closed in 1957.

The 19th century produced a number of events which were to have a great influence on the country in general. In 1801 the Act of Union, instigated by William Pitt as a means of solving the 'Irish problem', saw Ireland become part of the United Kingdom of Great Britain and Ireland. Although Irish Protestants were not entirely convinced that the Act of Union was desirable, the Catholic Emancipation Act in 1829 which allowed Catholics to sit in Parliament persuaded them that they would have a greater majority as part of Britain and they gave the Act their support. The Act of Union also resulted in the later formation of a number of societies such as the Young Irelanders and the Irish Republican Brotherhood, in the hope of breaking Ireland's connection with Britain.

During the 19th century the majority of Irish peasants depended on the potato for survival. In

# Light & Learning

1845 disease caused the potatoes to rot and the crop to fail, disaster followed in the form of the Great Famine of 1846. Fortunately for the people of Armagh(although a farming community), industries such as linen, fruit-growing and flour-milling helped them to survive and the Famine and it did not cause the same hardship as in other parts of Ireland where over a million people died of starvation and disease. However many joined another million who emigrated to countries like America.

The Famine was to affect Armagh in that the building of St. Patrick's R.C. Cathedral, begun in 1840 by Cardinal Crolly, eventually came to a halt as the collections made for its erection were diverted to famine relief and it was not until 1852 that work began again. The Cathedral was dedicated in 1873 but it was not until 1904 that it was finally consecrated.

The end of the 18th and beginning of the 19th century also saw the development of health care within the Armagh area. Although a Charitable Infirmary supported by private subscriptions was already in existence in 1765, an Act passed by the Irish House of Commons that year arranged for the provision of county hospitals and, after being housed within the Infirmary for some years, in 1774 the new County Infirmary was built at the top of Dawson Street.

During 1816 to 1818 an outbreak of typhus fever affected the area and Lady Molyneux of Castledillon set up a Fever Hospital on the outskirts of Armagh where it is said "the malady was more speedily eradicated than in any other town in Ireland." Unfortunately there was another outbreak of the disease in 1824 and the then Archbishop, Lord John George Beresford, built another Fever Hospital which was later to become the Macan Asylum for the Blind and, even later, housed the nuns and boarders of the Sacred Heart Convent when the convent was burned in the 1960's. Today the site is a housing estate on the Cathedral Road.

When the Bill for the Provision of the Lunatic Poor came into being in 1817 the Armagh District Asylum, now known as St. Luke's Hospital, was the first of its kind to be built under that Act and was designed by the celebrated architect, Francis Johnston. The foundation stone was laid in 1821 and the official opening took place in July 1825. At that time people considered to be mentally ill were detained in prisons but when Armagh became a County Asylum in 1863 a great number of these unfortunates were sent to the Armagh hospital. However, it appears that the staff were often a greater problem than the patients with housemaids described as "insolent", keepers had "bad tongues", cooks were "quarrelsome and incompetent" and laundry maids had "bad tempers".

Around this time the pioneering work of Florence Nightingale inspired many young women to follow a career in medicine and, one such woman was Dr. Dora Allman who was a doctor in Armagh County Asylum when the First World War broke out. During the war she acted as temporary superintendent while the manager, Dr. Lawless, was absent on military duties. She was described as "very capable and not easily intimidated" (Patterson) and this was proved when a strike was called which crippled all the Irish Mental Hospitals. All, that is, except Armagh. The story goes that when the staff went on strike leaving Dr. Allman to cope on her own she was undaunted, appealing to the Commanding Officer of the Royal Irish Fusiliers who sent a party of soldiers to cook meals and assist her in any way necessary.

The poor were very much with us in the 19th century and the Houses of Industry and Houses of Correction of the 17th century became the predecessors of the 19th century workhouses and unions. Poverty was seen to be the result of laziness and vagrants were punished for their problems, although Dean Swift, a frequent visitor to Armagh, believed that people would work if jobs were available. However, begging was considered almost a profession and the story goes that when Mary Smith, the daughter of two blind street beggars, was married in 1818 her mother gave her £50 and said she would have given her more "did she not fear the regulation lately made in the city would prevent street begging and spoil trade." A year later the 'Armagh Association for the Total Suppression of Street Begging' realised her fears.

In 1833 a Royal Commission was set up to look into the problem of poverty and showed that the problem was much worse in Ireland than in England and Wales. The Poor Law was introduced in 1838 whereby the country was divided into unions, each union having a workhouse, and the County Workhouse was built at Tower Hill in 1842.

Although the workhouse was intended to provide food and shelter in return for hard work, the thinking of the Government at the time was to deter people from using the facility by deliberately making the workhouse a terrible place and it was seen as a last resort by most people. Almost one hundred years later few able-bodied paupers used the establishment and it had become a refuge for the elderly and infirm. In 1908, with the introduction of the Old Age Pension and later unemployment and sickness benefits, the workhouse, as it was intended, had become obsolete and was closed in 1948.

But all was not doom and gloom during the 19th century in Armagh. Regardless of politics, poverty and the pursuit of business, some of the local populace found time for relaxation in the form of sport. The horse races that were popular in the 17th century still took place although meetings were held in other venues such as Ballynahonebeg, Milford and later at Farmacaffley where the annual point-to-point is still held.

Cricket continues to be played on The Mall since English troops introduced the game during the late 18th century. It became of great local interest when in 1845 Mr. Wiltshire, the then proprietor of the Beresford Arms Hotel, leased the central field and opened it to the public and in 1859 Armagh Cricket Club was founded and still flourishes.

Another game which flourished during the 19th century was 'bullets' or road bowls mentioned in a poem written by Dean Swift in 1728 as "long bullets". The game, which entails opponents throwing the bullet for as great a distance as possible along various country roads, is thought to have originated with Dutch soldiers during the 17th century and a similar game has been played in Holland since the 14th century. Immigrant weavers from Scotland and England are also credited with perpetuating the interest in bullets but in the first part of the 20th century the interest waned somewhat, except in two counties, Cork and Armagh. Today, however, road bowls is attracting great interest again, so much so that the International Championships rotate between Ireland, Germany and the Netherlands, attracting huge crowds whether played in Armagh, Cork or Amsterdam.

The 20th century has also brought about a new and better image for Armagh. No longer can one subscribe to the sentiments of a 13th century rhyme which described Armagh as follows:

"Armagh - 'tis a pity,
Is now a vain City,
Deprived of all common morality
The women go nude,

> The meat's taken crude,
> And poverty there has locality."

A description that is owed to the condition of a city continually ravaged by war.

Today Armagh might still be 'vain' but it is a vanity born of pride. The people of Armagh can be proud that their city has never succumbed to the burnings and destruction to which it has been subjected down through the centuries, even to the present day. Instead, by 1995, Armagh had risen like a Phoenix from the ashes to receive official city status once more and to celebrate over 1,550 years of Christianity.

The past is ever present and the future, in the shape of science and technology, helps bring that past to life within the Orchard County of Ireland - in Armagh, City of Light and Learning. Perhaps a more fitting rhyme for the 20th century would read:

> Armagh is uncowed,
> As a City she's proud
> Of a great past and a future unfurled,
> For out of the ashes,
> Despite constant clashes,
> Her beauty is known 'cross the world!

# Bibliography

Alexander, E., Lady Anne's Garden (London, 1903)
Bassett, G.H., County Armagh 100 Years Ago (Belfast, 1888, reprint, 1989)
Brett, C.E.B., Court houses and Market houses of the Province of Ulster (Belfast, 1973)
eds. Day, A., and McWilliams, P., Parishes of County Armagh 1835-1888 (Belfast, 1990)
Department of Environment, NI., Pieces of the Past (Belfast 1988)
Fitzgerald, D. and Weatherup, R., The Way We Were (Belfast, 1993)
ed. Foster, R.F., The Oxford Illustrated History of Ireland (Oxford, 1989)
Gray, T., Nationalist and Unionist Ireland before the Treaty (Edinburgh, 1993)
Keady Historical Society, Keady - Journal of Keady and District Historical Society (Armagh, 1992)
Kinsella, T., The Tain (Oxford, 1970)
Mallory, J.P., Navan Fort - the Ancient Capital of Ulster (Belfast)
Marshall, J.J., History of Charlemont Fort and Borough in the County of Armagh (Tyrone, 1921)
The National Trust, The Argory (Belfast, 1984)
NICLR, Navan Quest - a time journey of discovery. Educational pack. (Belfast)
O'Farrell, P., Ancient Irish Legends (Dublin, 1995)
Patterson, T.G.F., Armagh Miscellanea (Vol XI)
Patterson, T.G.F., Harvest Home (Dundalk, 1975)
Patterson, T.G.F., Hospital News (Vols. 2,4 & 5)
Scott, M., Irish Myths and Legends (London, 1994)
Stuart, J., Historical Memoirs of the City of Armagh (Dublin, 1900)
Weatherup, R., Armagh - Historic Photographs of the Primatial City (Belfast, 1993)
Armagh Guardian, Ulster Gazette and Armagh Observer (various editions)

# Acknowledgments

In writing about Armagh I have tried to project an overall picture of life in the city as it developed through the centuries. Many places and events have not been mentioned simply because it would take several books to give a detailed account of Armagh. I have relied heavily on the writings of the late T.G.F. Patterson, past curator of Armagh County Museum who it seems has explored every nook and cranny and every aspect of life in Armagh. I would like to thank Roger Weatherup, Mr. Patterson's able successor, who pointed me in the right direction and Mary McVeigh, who endeavoured to keep me on that path. My thanks also go to Bee Gordon, Dermot Kelly and the members of Crosscurrents, Anne Hart and Nick Sadlier at Navan, Paddy Pender and Emir Sheppard, the staff of Armagh County Museum and the staff of Armagh Branch Library, all of whom helped greatly with my research.

# Local directory and Sponsors

Cottage Publications would like to express their sincere thanks
to the following businesses and organisations without whose
help and support this book would not have been possible.

*Unless otherwise stated addresses are in Armagh City (Telephone code 01861)*

| NAME AND ADDRESS | TEL | FAX |
|---|---|---|
| *Apple Growers, Canners & Processors* | | |
| Glass Brothers, 132 Kilmore Road | 01762 851263 | 01762 852215 |
| *Armagh Observatory* | | |
| Armagh Observatory, College Hill | 522928 | 527174 |
| WWW Address: http://star.arm.ac.uk | | |
| *Artist* | | |
| The Studio of Joe Hynes, Portadown | 01762 332271 | |
| *Bar & Pub Food* | | |
| The Corner Bar, 1 Main Street, Hamiltonsbawn | 01762 871070 | |
| *Building Designers, Surveyors & Engineers* | | |
| Cornett Design Associates, 4 Hartford Place, The Mall | 523330 | 528808 |
| *City & District Council* | | |
| Armagh City and District Council, Council Offices, The Palace Demesne | 529600 | 529601 |

| Name and address | Tel | Fax |
|---|---|---|
| *Education* | | |
| The Royal School, College Hill | 522807/523196 | 511126 |
| Armagh College of Further Education, Lonsdale Street | 522205 | 526011 |
| The Queen's University at Armagh, 39 Abbey Street | 510678 | 510679 |
| *Estate Agents* | | |
| City Property Services, 31 Thomas Street | 528888 | 523584 |
| *Florist* | | |
| The Flower Bowl International, 66 Scotch Street | 522635 | 01762 339742 |
| *Gift Ideas & Period Doors* | | |
| Period Doors, 40 Scotch Street | 522359 | 522359 |
| *Hotel* | | |
| Charlemont Arms Hotel, 63-65 English Street | 522028 | 526979 |
| *Insurance Brokers* | | |
| T. A. Abbott & Sons Ltd, 18 Russell Street | 523163 | 524843 |
| Richhill Insurance, 2 New Line, Richhill | 01762 871597 | 01762 871597 |
| *Ladies Fashions* | | |
| T. J. Walker Ltd, 3-5 Market Street | 522181/2 | |
| *Lawnmower Sales* | | |
| Freeburn Lawnmowers, 28 Drumilly Road, Hockley | 01762 871747 | 01762 870730 |
| *Pharmacy* | | |
| Hills Chemist, 64-68 Market Street, Tandragee | 01762 840209 | 01762 840209 |

| Name and address | Tel | Fax |
|---|---|---|
| *Photographer* | | |
| Michael Campbell Photography, Mall West | 526120 | 528727 |
| *Post Office & Retail Outlet* | | |
| Armagh Post Office, 31 English Street | 510313 | |
| *Public Relations* | | |
| Maureen Campbell, Woodford Communications | 511445 | 526195 |
| *Quantity Surveyors & Building Consultants* | | |
| J. B. Kingston & Partners, 2 Rokeby Green, The Mall | 523661 | 526217 |
| *Soft Furnishing Retailer* | | |
| Wright's Soft Furnishings, 14 English Street | 523762 | 525585 |
| *Solicitors* | | |
| Brian W. Dougan LL.B., 6 Russell Street | 522724 | 523221 |
| W. G. Menary & Co., 4 Hartford Place, The Mall | 528900 | 528900 |
| *Stud & Racing Stables* | | |
| Dartan Ree, 3 Dartan Ree, Tynan | 568927 | 568837 |
| *Supermarket* | | |
| J. D. Hunter & Co., 3-5 The Square, Markethill | 551209 | 551195 |
| *Upholstery* | | |
| Annvale Upholstery, 20b Killylea Road | 510378 | |
| *Visitor Centre* | | |
| The Navan Centre, 81 Killylea Road | 525550 | 522323 |

Dear Reader

We hope you have found this book both enjoyable and useful. This is just one of our range of illustrated titles. Other areas currently featured include:–

Strangfords Shores
Dundalk & North Louth
The Mournes

Also available in our "Illustrated History & Companion Range" are:-

Ballycastle and the Heart of the Glens
Larne and the Road to the Glens
Coleraine and the Causeway Coast
City of Derry
Hillsborough
Ballymoney
Lisburn

Ballymena
Banbridge
Newtownards
Holywood
Bangor
Newry

The paintings featured in each of the titles above are also available as signed artists prints.

If you require any further information please call or fax us on (01247) 883876,
E-Mail us on cottage_publ@online.rednet.co.uk
or write to:–

**Cottage Publications**
**15 Ballyhay Road**
**Donaghadee, Co. Down**
**N. Ireland, BT21 0NG**